Turn Your
Cablight On

Turn Your Cablight On

Get Your Dream Man in 6 Months or Less

NANCY SLOTNICK

GOTHAM BOOKS

GOTHAM BOOKS

Published by Penguin Group (USA) Inc.
375 Hudson Street, New York, New York 10014, U.S.A.
Penguin Group (Canada), 90 Eglinton Avenue East, Suite 700, Toronto, Ontario
M4P 2Y3, Canada (a division of Pearson Penguin Canada Inc.); Penguin Books Ltd,
80 Strand, London WC2R 0RL, England; Penguin Ireland, 25 St Stephen's Green,
Dublin 2, Ireland (a division of Penguin Books Ltd); Penguin Group (Australia), 250
Camberwell Road, Camberwell, Victoria 3124, Australia (a division of Pearson Aus-
tralia Group Pty Ltd); Penguin Books India Pvt Ltd, 11 Community Centre,
Panchsheel Park, New Delhi - 110 017, India; Penguin Group (NZ), cnr Airborne and
Rosedale Roads, Albany, Auckland 1310, New Zealand (a division of Pearson New
Zealand Ltd); Penguin Books (South Africa) (Pty) Ltd, 24 Sturdee Avenue, Rose-
bank, Johannesburg 2196, South Africa

Penguin Books Ltd, Registered Offices: 80 Strand, London WC2R 0RL, England

Published by Gotham Books, a division of Penguin Group (USA) Inc.

First printing, January 2006
10 9 8 7 6 5 4 3 2 1

Gotham Books and the skyscraper logo are trademarks of Penguin Group (USA) Inc.

LIBRARY OF CONGRESS CATALOGING-IN-PUBLICATION DATA
has been applied for.

ISBN 1-592-40178-3

Printed in the United States of America
Set in Goudy and Goudy Sans Italic • Designed by Sabrina Bowers

Contents

Acknowledgments

There are a number of people who made this book happen and who helped me to discover my philosophy on dating strategy. First, I should probably thank every guy I ever dated (although there are a few I'm reluctant to thank) for teaching me about men through trial and error. I want to thank my clients, in particular the ones who contributed their stories and insights about my Program to this book. Their openness on this topic was extremely brave and I really appreciate it.

I want to recognize the people in my life who have helped to shape my perspective on dating and relationships, including Lois Mound, Cheryl Dollinger Brown, my friends and former partners in crime in the dating scene (most notably Lisa Bornstein), my sisters and my parents, and, of course, my husband, Daniel Aferiat, who has both directly and indirectly taught me so much about psychology, relationships, and the mysterious ways of men.

I would like to thank Britta Steiner Alexander, who believed in this book before it was conceived, and who was willing to take a chance on me before a single word was on paper. Britta—Your strength of vision, enthusiasm, energy, and faith were inspirational. The way that you "got me" was central to my decision to move forward and was such a support throughout the process. Thank you to Ned Leavitt also for believing in me and for trusting Britta! Thank you to Erin Bush Moore and Jessica Sindler and everyone at Gotham for your encouragement, editorial advice, and guidance, and for your responsiveness during the writing period. Erin—Thank you for fighting for the acquisition, even from overseas!

I am particularly grateful to Jennifer Wulff for her humor, style, and dedication to this book. Jen—Our instant chemistry served to cement the project. Your wit, patience, creativity, ability to listen, and sense of fun were instrumental in bringing my ideas to life. Thank you so much.

—Nancy

Turn Your
Cablight On

Introduction

Is everyone you know mystified that you're single? You're attractive, you're smart, you have a lot of friends and a successful career, so why has it been so hard to find a mate? Well, don't lose hope just yet. (You must have at least a small glimmer of it or you wouldn't be reading this.) Do you feel ready to make changes in your life in order to find yourself someone you like who likes you back, just the way you've always dreamed of? If so, I can help you. In my coaching practice, I've developed a series of steps that have helped my clients find the right guy for them, in 6 months or less. I can do the same for you. You need to be ready, though, and you've got to do the work. Nothing grueling and nothing embarrassing, but, just as you would when looking for an ideal job or a great apartment, you need to spend some time and effort to find your dream guy. Of course, the work is also fun, because you'll be getting more attention from men and having more dates! Before we start, I want you to ask yourself the same three questions that I tell my coaching clients to ask themselves before I start working with them:

1. Am I committed to finding someone? A lot of women will say a relationship is their Number One priority, but how much time are you willing to spend on the search?

2. Am I confident enough in myself to know I'm a great catch, but still able to look at myself in a critical way?
3. Am I ready to face my fears? Dating is all about taking risks, and you need to be prepared for rejection, whether you're on the receiving end or the giving end.

If you've answered yes to all three, keep reading.

IT'S OKAY TO ADMIT YOU WANT A MAN!

If you hesitated before buying this book, you're probably not alone. Women often feel embarrassed to admit they want their lovelives to be important. In a way, the women's movement did a disservice to our generation of women, because while we were encouraged to go after career goals, we were subtly discouraged from pursuing relationship goals. I'm not saying that we should go back to the days when women went to college for an MRS degree. However, it should not be embarrassing to want a great man as much as—or more than—you want a great job. We may not *need* men anymore for financial stability, but we still *want* them. You may be so over dating and rejection that you're telling yourself you're happy alone, but are you really?

If you're anything like I was when I was dating, you probably get a lot of advice from all sorts of people—your mom, your girlfriends, your coworkers. Sometimes nosy strangers will even try to offer you pointers. They probably give conflicting advice, too. Your girlfriend will say, "Sure, call him if you haven't heard from him!" while your mom says that if he doesn't call you every single day, he's a worthless cad. If you're ready for some good advice, and advice that's proven to work, I want you to stop listening to everyone else and start listening to your new dating coach: me.

MY BACKGROUND

I've always been intrigued by people's lovelives. After graduating from Harvard, where I majored in psychological anthropology, I became a headhunter in New York City. It was a great career and something I was good at, but one day, I realized I was often more interested in my clients' lovelives than their careers. Being a headhunter just wasn't my true calling. I wanted to be in the business of helping people find love. So, I left my job to start my own dating service, in the form of a café on Manhattan's Upper West Side. We sold coffee and beer and wine, and even served great comfort food like Rice Krispies Treats and milk and cookies, but the main draw was that people would fill out a dating profile, in hopes that someone would want to be set up on a date with them. The name? Drip. (Because everyone feels like a Drip when they're dating!) I saw 35,000 people fill out profiles, and there were hundreds of marriages as a result. All the first dates happened at Drip, which was a lot of fun to watch. When couples got engaged, they would often come back to the place they first met and tell me their stories. That was my favorite part. There's nothing like knowing you had a hand in helping someone meet their soul mate. After watching so many people walk off into the sunset together, I finally took the time and the steps to look for a guy for myself. Once those steps worked for me, I wanted to share all that I had learned with others, so I started my own coaching practice.

Now it's your turn to find a great guy. And I want to help you do it. The reason why I wanted to write this book is that I wish I could have had some of this advice when I was dating. I would have saved myself so much time and heartache. Whatever your reasons were for buying this book—whether you feel like you've hit rock bottom and need help, or you were just intrigued by the cover—you've come to the right place.

Clients often come to me when dating has become a source of stress in their lives. But if you start following my Program before you get to that point, you can avoid that stress, or at least keep the anxiety to a minimum. I can save you on the time and heartache. Even if you're just dating for fun at the moment and not ready for something long-term, the tools and tricks I'm about to teach you will be invaluable as you go forward in your lovelife. To me, it's like knowing a shortcut. You can sit in traffic and be miserable, or do it the easy way by listening to someone who knows better. I can help you get to a relationship faster. And not just any relationship, but a *healthy* relationship.

WHY *Cablight*?

So, how is this book different from the rest on the dating shelf? The problem with most of the books already out there is that they oversimplify things. As you've probably realized, dating is far from simple. You can't boil everything down to a set of *Rules* or a blanket statement like *He's Just Not That into You.* The answer is: It's complicated. Becoming successful at dating—with the end goal of a long-term relationship—means you need to learn more than a catchphrase. You need to know how to read men and how to understand their language, as well as how to read your own behaviors and feelings. You'll find it's easy once you have the tools, but there are many steps to take first. Yep, I'm going to put you to work in this Program. No more taking the easy way out. Just as you can't just read an exercise book and expect to get in shape, you can't just read my book and think you're immediately going to get a guy. You need to do the work. But once you put what I say into practice, you *will see results*.

NO MORE EXCUSES!

As your coach and cheerleader, I don't want to hear any more excuses for why you're not having any luck with dating. Whether it's out of self-defense or denial, if you say things to yourself like "Men suck" or "Guys don't like girls like me" or "I'm so unique, nobody 'gets me,'" you have to stop that! These statements won't help you get to your goal. I know that it's hard. And I know that it's not fair that you have to work at finding someone. You wonder, "Why is it that love just lands in the lap of so many other people?" But I'll tell you the same thing I tell my clients: Do you want it to be fair, or do you want to be happy? There's no point in pitying yourself. Don't be the victim. Not when it's in your power to do something about it. You can create your own luck. It's time to take charge of your lovelife! That's right—once you start this Program and learn to turn on your Cablight, things are going to turn around.

So . . . Are you ready to be happy?

Turn Your Cablight On

W*hat does it mean* to turn your Cablight on? There is a certain glow, or an aura if you will, that you need to exude in order to attract the right guy. It lets men know that you are approachable. It's not about dressing slutty or actually asking a guy out. It's more subtle than that. Think available, not desperate. Women often think it seems desperate to be on a manhunt at all, but if you don't put yourself "on the market," guys won't know you're available. I liken it to a cablight. I was trying to get a cab one day near my apartment in Manhattan, and wasn't having any luck. In New York City, you know when a cabbie is looking for a fare because his light is on, so I didn't even bother raising my hand for all the unavailable, unlit cabs going by. But then it occurred to me: What if one of them had a broken light and the driver didn't know it? He'd be driving all over the city looking for someone to hail him, but no one would. Why? Because he was sending the wrong signal, inadvertently. Could it be that your own light is off? You *think* you've been looking, but because you don't appear to be available—emotionally or otherwise—no guy has flagged you down. I'm going to help you find that light and turn it on. Whether you're showing your vulnerable side, your flirtatious side, or your seductive side, the point is to make it easy for a man to talk to you. Men are as afraid of rejection as we are, so if you make a guy feel like he won't be shot down, your odds of him hailing you are much better. Once you've learned how to turn your Cablight on, you can end your dating drought for good and find the relationship you've always hoped for, all within the next 6 months.

Sometimes, it can help to hear from women who have been through my Program already, so I've asked some of my clients to share their own experiences and thoughts with you. You'll see a lot of what they have to say throughout the book, under the heading "In My Clients' Words."

MAKE THE 15-HOUR COMMITMENT

In My Clients' Words

Whenever I go out now, I remind myself to turn my Cablight on. I went to a speed-dating event last night and remembered to smile at everyone and use my body language, and I thought I did pretty well. I just logged onto the site where you see who wants to go out with you again, and nine out of ten guys picked me as a "yes"! —Samantha

Of course, in addition to putting your Cablight on, you also have to be on duty. You're not going to meet anyone if you don't put some time into finding someone. Comparing looking for a guy to looking for a job is a common analogy because although you don't want to go after a guy with the same aggressive intensity that

---

Is This Your Typical Saturday?

To-Do List
- Buy baby shower gift for Danielle
- Clean bathroom
- Write thank-you note to Heidi
- Drop clothes off at Goodwill
- Bake cookies for office party
- Call Mom
- Buy a dress for Susan's wedding
- Organize closet
- Oh—find a boyfriend

---

you would that executive account manager job (you don't want to scare him!), you do need to spend a lot of time on the search. How much time? 15 hours. *Per week*. Did your eyes just pop out of your head? A lot of my clients' do when I tell them the number of hours I require in order for my Program to work for them. But again, if you were out of work, you'd spend at least that much time searching for a job, right? You'd send out résumés, start networking, go to industry events, contact old friends . . . And you wouldn't know which of these would pan out until you tried. Somehow, when it comes to relationships, people don't think it should take that kind of time and effort. They want Tom Cruise to just land on their doorstep, engagement ring in hand and down on one knee. But it doesn't happen that way. Unless you're Katie Holmes.

The other thing I tell people who can't imagine spending 15 hours on the search is, if they *did* meet a great guy, wouldn't they want to spend 15 hours a week with him? You have to make room for him in advance. Yes, in order to find him, you might have to cut back on the number of hours you spend watching *The Bachelor,* but wouldn't you rather be out there finding your own bachelor than enduring yet another "most dramatic rose ceremony ever"? Or are you the type who never has time for TV, overextending yourself and rushing around without ever stopping to smell the roses? Well, now is the time to slow down and start sniffing around.

CLEAR YOUR PLATE

Nature abhors a vacuum, and if I can only walk with
sufficient carelessness I am sure to be filled.
—HENRY DAVID THOREAU

The more room you leave for something to happen in your life, the more easily it will happen. Think of a sealed plastic bottle from which all the air has been sucked out. As soon as you make even the smallest hole, air will rush in. There's a physics principle that says that nature abhors a vacuum. Don't fight nature! You need to leave room for good things to happen to you. If you overschedule yourself, you're leaving no room for anything or anyone to enter into your life. If you are always running late and rushing from commitment to commitment, there is no time for serendipity. While you do need to be busy in your quest to find someone in your 15 hours per week, you also want to leave the chance for something spontaneous to happen. Drop the faux commitments. Instead of baking cookies to bring to that party, buy them. Consider skipping the next baby shower. Screw the thank-you notes! Take a leisurely walk, window-shop, or sit and read on a park bench instead, all the while being aware of your surroundings. You never know who might come strolling along. If you're running around like an overbooked crazy lady, you may rush past that cute guy trying to ask you for the time of day. Start caring about yourself as much as you care about others.

PRIORITIZE

As they say in the lottery, "You've got to be in it to win it." Most women say that finding a meaningful relationship is the most important priority in their lives. Yet very few will spend much time or money on it. These same women might fork over hundreds or even thousands of dollars on every new style of Jimmy Choo shoes, but they balk at the $20 a month it costs for an online dating site membership. Or they'll say they want a relationship to happen "the natural way" and that they shouldn't have to work at finding it. But what do they mean by "the natural way"? Is it more natural to go out with a guy who sits next to you on an airplane? Why is that more natural than dating online? Resolving to meet someone "the natural way" is nothing more than a rationalization to be passive about your lovelife. By putting yourself in situations to make finding a guy easier, you're simply playing smart. And you have to, these days! Fate still plays a role, but why not make things easier on yourself by meeting it in the middle? Some of you may be saying, "Well, I've tried putting myself 'out there' and it didn't work, so I'm not going to do that again." Yes, you are! The difference is that I'm going to tell you how to do it the *right* way. No more just going through the motions! You'll see that, when you learn how to date using my strategy, you *will* get results. Not just in the quantity of guys you go out with, but also in the quality. We're talking grade-A, take-home-to-Mom-and-call-the-caterer guys, who are also sexy and fun. Believe it or not, you'll soon have a choice of whom you date.

Part of the Cablight principle is to give off energy—that's what leads men to come to you. Being open is what attracts men. Being closed doesn't. So, as you start this Program, be open to everything, whether it's talking to that guy in front of you in the ATM line or your mom setting you up with her hairdresser's son. You could miss something great because you're being too closed-minded about who you're looking for or where you might find him.

WHAT'S URGENT AND WHAT'S IMPORTANT?

There's this saying about priorities that I like a lot: "Know the difference between what's important and what's urgent, and do what's important first." Counterintuitive, right? For instance, your boss might be calling you on your cell phone, but a cute guy is approaching you at the same time. What's more urgent? The boss, of course. But what's more important? The guy! It's amazing how often urgent things can actually wait. What could be more important than a guy you like? You have to teach yourself to make the Search for a Man a true priority.

GO ON ONE DATE A WEEK

When some of my clients start coming to me, they question how they're going to get a date every week, but they soon find that it just starts happening. As you keep reading, you'll see how it isn't going to be a problem for you, either, as long as your Cablight is on and you're putting in your 15 hours. The reason why I want you to go on a date a week is not only for the obvious goal of trying to find the right guy. By dating often, you're going to become better at dating, for one. You'll also get over your fear of rejection, which is a huge roadblock for most women. Rather than wallowing in it, you'll start taking a more practical approach to being both the rejecter and the rejectee. It's not some earth-shattering thing! When you go on one date every two months, there's a tendency to pin too much hope—and pressure—on the date. When you have one date a week, it's no big deal if it's a dud. Ultimately, you're only looking for one person. You can't expect to connect with everyone. It's best to think of it like two pieces of a puzzle: You are trying to see if you fit. Over time, your instincts will improve, too. Instead of taking four dates to realize if a guy is good for you, you'll start to know it in one. You'll be able to "name that tune" in fewer notes!

> *When you go on a date a week, you start to realize that there's always another guy around the corner. You get so much stronger as a result. I always grasped so hard onto every guy I went out with, and now I can let things go much more easily. —Debbie*

In My Clients' Words

SO, WHY NOT TWO OR FIVE DATES A WEEK?

I've found that one date a week seems to be the right balance for most women. Two or more a week, and you start losing your ability to judge a guy on his own merit. You begin pitting your men against each other and risk overlooking someone great in the process. When you think you have too many options, you usually end up playing things a little too cool. One client of mine forgot to call a great guy back that she'd met at a bar because she had a "better" prospect lined up later in the week. A few months later she ran into him again and realized she'd missed out on something good.

HAVE FUN!

More than anything else in this Program, I want you to have fun. Dating has become this awful chore, a means to an end. But it's not such bad homework going on a date a week or starting a conversation with the guy behind you in line at Starbucks. If you're making these situations too stressful, you're probably taking things too seriously. I'll help you with that as we get going. Remember, too, that every date is a good date, even if it's horrible, because it's putting you one step closer to the right guy for you. As I learned from working in sales, "Every no leads you closer to a yes." And most women take something home with them from every date anyway, whether it's learning not to overshare about past relationships or knowing to stick to just one martini and not three. Or maybe you'll just have a good time being out.

In my dating days, I had what I call "the perfect date with the wrong guy." I got asked out to dinner by a guy, but the place where we wanted to go had a long wait. We were trying to figure out somewhere else to go and he just turned to me and said, "Do you want to just pick up some sandwiches and go to the beach?" We were in Manhattan and, living there, I didn't even know how to get to a beach! So we got in his 4x4 and drove to Long Island. The weather was gorgeous, so we had the windows open and I remember the song "How Bizarre" playing on his CD player. We got a bottle of wine and sat on the sand while watching the

---

Silver Linings

Dark Cloud: He talked about his lawn care system the whole
  time.
Silver Lining: I can't wait to try that fertilizer he recommended!

Dark Cloud: That guy was so arrogant, I could barely take it!
Silver Lining: Maybe finding a guy who looks like a Calvin Klein
  model isn't that important to me after all.

Dark Cloud: That date would not end. I can't believe I got roped
  into dinner with him when we were just planning to meet for
  drinks.
Silver Lining: I'm going to practice how to say no to people.

Dark Cloud: He wouldn't take his hands off me. As if I'd sleep
  with him on the first date!
Silver Lining: I guess I should learn to read online profiles better.
  The fact that he goes by the name PussyLover and says that he
  hates cats might have been my first clue.

---

surf roll in. I ended up not really liking him in the end, but that
date was so perfect regardless.

Bottom line: Dating really should be fun. After all, it's free
dinner (most of the time)! It's putting on a cute outfit, going
out, and having a new adventure. This isn't digging ditches,
girls. Whether you end up liking the guy or not, it's a chance to
try a new restaurant, explore a new neighborhood, maybe do a
fun activity, like skeet shooting or rock climbing, that you
might never have tried otherwise. You'll get to know men much

better, too. The more you understand men and how they think, the better prepared you'll be for the relationship you do end up finding at the end of all this. Each time you go out with a man, you learn more and more about *men*, if you're paying attention. Above all, think positive! If you go into this Program with a "This sucks" attitude, it really *is* going to suck. Watch out for self-fulfilling prophesies like that. (If you think you'll live your whole life alone, you just might.) Sometimes it helps to think of dating as a scavenger hunt where you know the prize is out there somewhere—you just have to find it. In the meantime, enjoy the wild ride!

something that is really a deal-breaker for you, stop going out with him. Some behaviors might simply be intolerable for you, and it's perfectly fine to hold out for someone else.

But if you want to use my Strategy to find the One, no more comments like "There are no good men out there" or "Men are pigs" or "All the great ones are gay." In fact, there's a lot about men that women can learn from, as you'll see in chapter six.

YOUR DATING RÉSUMÉ

To get an idea of a new client's dating patterns, I start by asking four questions:

1. How old are you?
2. How often do you date?
3. How many serious relationships have you been in?
4. How many times have you been in love?

What were your answers? I'm always surprised to see how different the numbers are for answers 3 and 4. You would think they'd be the same, but so many women have either not been in love when they were in a serious relationship or not been in a serious relationship when they were in love. Often, the reason for the disparity in these two answers can be blamed on the bad patterns women fall into in relationships. I want you to write down a list of men from your past and how long each relationship lasted and why it ended. Try to get a little deeper than "I was late for lunch and he freaked out." It can't be *all* his fault.

Now study your list. Do you see any patterns? Do all your relationships end for the same reason? Take a look at the

Who	When	Why It Ended

following profiles and see if they fit you. If you're having trouble remembering why a relationship ended, or you're not seeing a pattern, ask your closest friends to help. They might have a better grasp on your dating history than you do.

The Control Freak

Are you the type who always tells a cabdriver which route to take? You think nothing of handing out your business card or asking men out? Do you tell a guy what time to call you back when you leave him a message, then get mad if he calls at a different time? If so, do the men in your life eventually stop returning your calls? It's because you've scared them away by being controlling. You probably made all the forward moves in the relationship, as well. This can only last a certain amount of time before one or both of you becomes tired of your roles. And before he starts to feel like he's on a leash.

The Serial Monogamist

Serial monogamists are usually pleasers. You have a hard time saying no to anyone. You go on dates with people you don't really like, often more than once. Or you might go after guys who borrow money from you and are otherwise not good enough. It's also rare that you are *not* in a relationship. Instead of ending something you're not that into, you stick around out of obligation or because it's comfortable. You know Newton's law? "Objects at rest tend to remain at rest unless an equal and opposite force acts upon them." I think relationships work the same way. Most people stay in a relationship unless there is some impetus to break up; for example, if they have to move for their jobs or someone happens to cheat or meet someone else. This is not good strategy! *You* can be the opposite force yourself through sheer will and this Program. Pleasers will even marry people they're not in love with, just because it's easier than "hurting them," and easier than getting back in the dating scene. One of the things you're going to learn from this book is how to say no to what you don't want. As important as learning how to face rejection is learning how to dish it out.

The Serial Dater

Ahhh, so many men, so little time. If you've set your standards so high that you keep jumping from guy to guy hoping for someone better without giving anyone half a chance, you're a serial dater. You want your relationships to be effortless, and you set a perfectionistic standard for the men in your life. You like to keep your options open and you have a hard time choosing one over another. If you ever want to be happy, you're going to have to break the cycle.

The Wallflower

Are you too passive when it comes to men? You don't go out in hopes that the right guy will somehow find you? Or when you do go out, you sit in the corner while your friends do all the flirting and talking? You probably also complain that nobody likes you and/or life sucks. Nobody likes you because they don't know you're there. It's time to come out of your shell.

Player Daters

Girls like you are into the bad-boy rock stars. Players are good at bringing out the sexy side in a girl, but it's very hard to keep those guys around. The instant-gratification factor is tempting, because it's so easy and titillating, but relationships like these rarely go anywhere. It's not to say you shouldn't date guys you have great chemistry with or who are hot, but going for sex appeal alone can lead to misery, especially if the guy is not able to be faithful. Guys who are players don't usually change their tune, even if you manage to get them all the way to the altar.

Sluts (Would You Prefer "Fun Loving"?)

There's nothing wrong with getting yourself a little something here and there, but if you consistently give it up too easily and most of your relationships can be counted in terms of hours rather than days, then you need to allow yourself to ask for more. If you constantly take crumbs from guys, that's all you're going to get. Your sexuality comes from within, not from random guys you hook up with. Chances are, you are thinking that sex will hook the guy in, or that it is somehow a replacement for the intimacy that you really want.

Now you might be thinking that each pattern or problem

requires a different solution. But the bottom line for all of you is: STOP IT! You can't keep these patterns and change your dating life at the same time. It doesn't fit in with the Strategy. I know that doesn't sound very sympathetic, but sometimes you've gotta give yourself some tough love. Be aware of the patterns you fall into and try to fight them every step of the way as you go through this book. It's going to be hard at times, but as long as you're conscious of the mistakes you've made in the past, you're going to have a much more promising future. There's a great saying I like to share with my clients whenever they continue on a path that won't likely lead anywhere: "If you always do what you've always done, you'll always get what you always got." And remember that if you're struggling with breaking bad patterns or having a hard time with anything else in my Program, I do offer one-on-one coaching.

GENDER ROLES

Gender roles are so ambiguous these days. With terms like "friends with benefits" and "fuck buddies" in common use, men are sometimes confused about what we might want out of a

---

In the following chapters, you'll see some deeper insights on dating and relationships from Daniel Aferiat, a licensed psychotherapist with a private practice in New York City. I find his advice to be so insightful when it comes to relationships, I even refer my clients to him sometimes when they need a little extra help. Of course, I'm biased, since he's also my husband. But he really knows his stuff!

Advice from Dan Aferiat, Your On-Call Therapist

Do you keep making the same mistakes with men?

It is a universal drive to replicate childhood patterns. Essentially, when people enter adult relationships they tend to repeat what they experienced as children in an attempt to master something that felt out of control. It's what Freud termed the "repetition compulsion." Dating can make you feel helplessly dependent. Whenever you invest in another person, you lose control. You can't control another person's actions and you can't make someone like you. What you can control is how you respond to your own thoughts and feelings. You'll be more capable of breaking patterns if you're aware that you fall into them.

relationship and even what they might want. They'll often go with whatever's easiest, so the more clear you can be about what kind of girl you are, without explicitly saying it, the better. Show your boundaries. If you want a guy to want more than sex from you, you can't send mixed signals by being too forward sexually. The same goes with being the pursuer in the relationship. If you're always doing the asking out, you can't suddenly be upset that he never calls. Not when you've beaten him to the punch from the start. If you want a man to pursue you, you have to let him. As much as gender roles have changed, a lot has remained traditional. Most women like to be pursued and most men like to be the pursuers. Go with it.

ROLE REVERSAL

There are, of course, the few rare women who prefer being in the "man role." They like making all the decisions in a relationship and being the pursuer. They'll plan all the vacations, decide when and where they'll go to dinner, and what to do for anniversary dates. But then you can't have it both ways. If you're always the one making the plans, it sets a precedent for the future. Most women like being pursued and romanced, and they like being surprised. If you're one of those 99%, you have to let him do things his way and in his own time. This doesn't

> *I always thought badly of men because I thought they had so much power to choose who they want to date, and that I had none. It was actually kind of sexist of me. Now, I feel like I'm in control, because if a guy doesn't return my gaze or choose to catch my hints, I just move on. It's oddly liberating to be, like, "Next!" Getting to that place has been . . . the final frontier for me. —Liz*

In My Clients' Words

mean you're a lesser person in the relationship. You're not being passive; you can still drop hints. It simply means you're letting him play a role you might appreciate later on, even if it makes you feel more vulnerable in the initial stages. Believe it or not, you're ultimately in the more powerful position.

BE THE NAVIGATOR

If you force a guy to do something your way, he might be doing it just because it's easier or because he doesn't want to have an argument. If you hint around instead and lead him in a certain direction, whether it's the first time you're meeting or your twentieth year of marriage, you will get your way more often. Think of him as the driver in the relationship, and yourself as the navigator. Just because you're in the passenger seat doesn't mean you have no control over where you're going! For instance, if you can manage to guide a guy into asking you for your number, isn't that a much better strategy than offering it outright—or worse, asking for his? First of all, he won't think your number is worth much if you just hand it out freely, and he'll question whether he ever wanted it to begin with. Secondly, men like to be "the man" and you have to honor that if you want to play smart in dating. You're emasculating them if you take their job away. And if he doesn't take the lead? Then you are smart to cut your losses and move on. You can't force it.

I'm going to go over a number of ways in which you should let him be the man. But in the initial stage of dating, it basically means letting him initiate the asking out, the calling, and more of the paying. It also means not trying to take back control by calling him the day after a date. Hold out and sit tight. It's worth the payoff.

SO, WHAT'S MY ROLE AS THE WOMAN?

Lure him in by flirting. Entice him with your personality and your sexuality. Do this by being subtly sensual, not overtly sexual. A lot of younger guys grew up with very blurred gender roles and they don't know what it means to date. You need to guide the progression of things by not "hooking up" with guys in your group of friends or with someone at work with the thought that it's going to lead to more than that. Try to lead the situation to a real date, instead. Courtship is a lost art, but it's easier than you think to bring it back. You can give strong hints. In desperate times, it's even okay to tell a male friend who might not catch on that you'd like more from him by saying, "So when are you going to ask me out?" It's a bold move and you have to be prepared for him to reject you, but if you don't want any regrets about him not knowing you're interested, that's a good way to do it. It's better than having things so ambiguous between you that you never know where you stand. It's flirtatious without being too demanding.

DON'T MAKE TWO MOVES IN A ROW

While it's important to let the guy be the pursuer, the magic in saying something like "You know I've got a crush on you" or "So when are you going to ask me out?" is that you're still letting him be the guy and giving him the space he needs to decide for himself what he wants. Also, you only say it once. Do not say a variation of the same thing the following week if he hasn't responded. That'll turn you from cute flirt to obsessive psycho girl. Think of statements like that as a one-time-use wild card. It's never a good idea to make two moves in a row because you'll come off as pushy and controlling and you'll be taking away his role. If he didn't respond to move #1, he's probably not interested, or he's just too chicken. Either way, you have to let it go. He will appreciate the space and respect you, no matter what the outcome. What I like to say is, "Keep your hopes high, but your expectations low." Unfortunately, the reason he hasn't asked you out yet could be that he's just not looking for the same thing as you are (i.e., a relationship). And, yes, he very well could be "not that into you." But, as you'll see, you can't fall back on that excuse every time. Not when it's in your power to *get* so many guys into you!

Having your Cablight on means exuding openness and confidence. You might have to do some soul-searching on what this means for you. You might also have to change a few things in your life in order to feel good about yourself and to be ready to get into the dating scene. It could be as simple as getting a new haircut or a hot new pair of jeans. Or it could be more complicated than that. Perhaps there's a codependent friendship you have that's bringing you down and holding you back. Maybe there are some demons from your past that you have to rid yourself of, bad relationships you need to get past mentally so that you can move on to more fulfilling ones. If anything is preventing you from tapping into your inner glow, including the bad patterns we went over in the last chapter, you need to take steps to fix it before you're going to have any success in my Program.

Sit down and think about "The Party That Is You," as I like to call it. Or the movie of your life. If you were looking at your life from the outside, how would you want it to be, versus how it is? Would you want to get to know you better if you were someone else? Would you be jealous of yourself? Would you date you if you were a guy? What distinguishes you from everyone else and makes you special? When someone is getting to know you, he's also getting to know himself because you're bringing something out in him that no one else does. In order to bring out his best, you need to give your best. When you meet strangers, it's natural to have your defenses up, but part of turning your Cablight on means letting down your guard a little. You have nothing to lose and everything to gain by giving someone a peek inside yourself. So what if you like Barry Manilow and old *Star Trek* reruns? It's embarrassing, sure, but that's good! These are the things that make you you.

One couple who met through my dating café, Drip, knew they were right for each other right away when they took a drive and a really cheesy seventies song came on the radio. They both started singing to it and got that giddy feeling you get when you really connect with someone, when you're laughing so hard you fall off your chair. That's gold! But you'll never have those moments if you don't belt out your own songs.

There's a great scene in the movie *My Best Friend's Wedding*. Julia Roberts strong-arms Cameron Diaz's character into singing karaoke, thinking that Cameron's fiancé (whom Julia's character is in love with) would be turned off after hearing her horrendous singing voice. Cameron belts out her off-key performance so

---

In My Clients' Words

All my life, I felt like I was on the disabled list of dating and that I had no power to change that. But I had this realization one day, after starting the Program with Nancy, that all my feelings about not being successful were self-imposed. What was holding me back was my own fear of moving forward and diving in. That's something I still need to remind myself of sometimes—not to retreat and hide but to really open up to the possibility of something good happening in my life. I constantly remind myself now that I am a catch! —Christina

sweetly and shamelessly, it actually endears her all the more to the guy. It's okay not to be perfect. When you're so stiff that you're not showing your personality, that's going to be far more of a turnoff than any dorky qualities you might possess. It's always better to show more of yourself than less. Embrace your dorkiness!

USE YOUR EYES

The first strategy to flirting is eye contact. But there's a fine line between a seductive glance and a psychotic stare! Even more important than knowing when to look at a guy is knowing when to look away. You should be the one to break first, but hold the look a little longer than you usually do. This is going to take a little practice, and you may want to try it on a few guinea pig guys if you're doing all this for the first time. But I promise: The difference between being the girl who's always approached and the one who isn't lies in perfecting your eye contact.

The next time you see a guy you're interested in, try to catch his gaze. Not by waving your arms or dancing on a banquette like you're

For some help in learning the art of eye contact, I often recommend watching some movies from the 1940s, where screen sirens like Rita Hayworth and Lauren Bacall had to rely more on eye contact and facial expressions to get across what they wanted to say (unlike in today's films, where they show a lot more skin). Turn the sound off and see how they flirt with their facial expressions. Directors used more close-ups then, so you can catch all the nuances of every performance and learn to use them yourself.

Quick Tip

Practice the "eye contact game" on the street. As you notice men walking past you, make eye contact and try to get them to check you out. Notice the way that the timing of the eye contact needs to be just right, as well. See what works. You'll be surprised to see how many guys play this game. Even the ones walking with women!

Tara Reid after a few too many Red Bulls, but just by trying to lock in his eyes with yours. Once he looks your way, he's going to see you checking him out. Do not give him a head-to-toe once-over, lick your lips, or otherwise act like you're in a Playboy pay-per-view special. You simply want to intrigue him, not make him think he's about to get laid. As far as how long to look, it's around two to three seconds. Just *past* the point of being comfortable. Then look away. But not in an abrupt "Sorry I was staring" kind of way. More of a reluctant "Oops, you caught me checking you out and I'm embarrassed" kind of way, topped with a little smile. This will become more second nature once you try it a few times. If all this is completely foreign, practice in the mirror. Sure, you're going to feel like a Drip, but better you feel like a Drip at home than at a crowded bar.

LOOK VULNERABLE, NOT WEAK

The key is to look vulnerable and sultry at the same time. It's true that the eyes are the window into the soul. Not only do you want to try to peek into his soul, you want to let him see into yours. But when I say "vulnerable," I don't mean you should

Cablight Props

When you're going out with the hope of meeting someone, bring or wear something that's a good conversation starter. A few ideas:

- A candy necklace (a nostalgic conversation piece, and it'll make him want to bite you)
- The *New York Times* crossword puzzle, but look up often so he can offer to help
- Animal crackers
- A sports team T-shirt. (If you're in New York and up for a friendly debate, try wearing a Red Sox tee.)
- A T-shirt with a cheeky saying, like "Flavor of the Week." (Stay away from anything too tongue-in-cheek, like "Your Boyfriend Wants Me," which Paris Hilton once wore.)
- A playbill for a show you just saw
- A gadget of any kind. Try the latest Game Boy or PlayStation Portable for best results.
- A how-to guide on playing poker and/or a deck of cards
- A water gun or other toy weapon. Men like weapons. (Make sure it's a toy.)

look weak in any way. If you look too vulnerable without looking like you know what you're up to, it can turn you into a victim. No deer in the headlights! Basically, you want to smile with your eyes. Try to smile without using your mouth. Try this in the mirror, too. Widen your eyes and raise your eyebrows a little until you're giving a warm, engaging gaze. One of my clients knew she had become a master at turning on her Cablight when she was walking down the street and got asked out right then and

---

Things That Aren't Conversation Starters

- A Prada turtleneck. Women might notice, but to guys . . . it's just a shirt that covers a lot of you.
- Polarizing T-shirts or buttons, like " 'No' Is a Whole Sentence!"
- Spreadsheets—You're out to have fun, so leave the work at home and look like you *can* have fun!
- Any book with the word "Depression" in the title

---

there by a guy she'd made eye contact with. He stopped her and said, "Come have a drink with me right now!"

THE IMPORTANCE OF BEING OPEN

How do you usually react if a guy uses a pickup line on you? If you're rude to him, you're not being open. Maybe he's nervous and that's the only way that he's ever known to start a conversation with a girl. Of course it's fine to turn someone down if you know you're completely not interested. But if it's your standard move to roll your eyes when a guy asks you if you "come here often," you're not only shutting him out, you're also shutting out any other guy who happened to see this exercise in humiliation. You're also not respecting how hard the guy's job is—to be the one doing the asking.

Even if a construction worker whistles at you, is there any harm in turning to smile? He complimented you! Sure, it wasn't welcome or necessary, but being more open and warm in situations like that is good practice. And, you get to see how a guy responds when you *do* acknowledge him. It's a whole different experience if you are used to being the ice queen. For example, when a guy asks you what time it is, that's often a pickup line. He is trying to strike up conversation. That's why there's the expression, "She wouldn't even give me the time of day."

UNWANTED ATTENTION

When you put your Cablight on, you will get a lot of attention, especially in the beginning. So be prepared. But the more you learn to be strategic with your Cablight beam, the more likely you are to get the attention you want rather than the kind you don't want. Unwanted attention should not be a deterrent to putting your Cablight on. It's just part of the job. It's like celebrities who complain about paparazzi. That unwanted attention is why they're getting paid millions and adored by all. You have to take the bad with the good. Suck it up and pretend you're Julia Roberts. On the other hand, if you're not getting any attention, you might need to kick things up a notch by dressing a little sexier than you normally do or expanding your flirting repertoire. If you're getting attention but are meeting more guys who want to take you home to bed instead of home to Mom, you probably need to tone down your sex appeal.

The best line a guy used on me was on New Year's Eve. We'd been checking each other out from across the room, and when he came over, he said, "What do you say we just start making out and if we don't like it, we'll stop?" It was right before midnight, so I had to laugh—and give him a kiss. It was one of my favorite New Year's Eves ever! —Toni

In My Clients' Words

SAFETY FIRST?

While we're on the topic of unwanted attention, a lot of people ask me about safety when I tell them they should have their Cablights on at all times. I ask them to consider whether the safety issue is just an excuse. Sure, it might not make me popular or PC to say that, but seriously, are you really putting your life in danger by smiling at someone? I am concerned for your safety, of course, but when someone makes too much out of it, it's often a defense mechanism. They're afraid of rejection, either giving it or taking it. Don't do anything stupid, of course. You don't want to invite a total stranger over to your apartment, nor should you meet someone for a date in a dark, secluded neighborhood. But how unsafe is it to give your cell phone number to someone, especially if they don't have your last name? If they don't know where you live, what's the danger? You're getting way ahead of yourself if you're imagining this person to be a stalker or a serial killer. You may be annoyed by the guy's advances, but that's a lot different than being in danger. You can always ignore his phone calls.

There are all kinds of fears associated with taking risks. But you need to take risks in order to get onto someone's radar. It doesn't mean you shouldn't use your brain. Don't get so wildly drunk, for instance, that you can't use your judgment. Don't give your last name to people at first meeting, and don't go anywhere alone with someone you've just met. You can easily avoid all those things while still taking some chances.

WHOA, WHERE'S THE DIMMER?!

Some people always have their Cablights on too bright. Either they rely too much on sexuality and don't play up their other attributes, or they come on too strong in the first few minutes of meeting a guy. If it's a relationship you're after, you need to send the right signal that will have a lasting effect.

One client of mine didn't even know she had her light on too bright. She's in her early thirties and was on a date with a guy who's a bit older than she is. There was another guy at the bar who was a *lot* older and not that desirable (let's just say he was a Newt Gingrich look-alike). While her date was in the bathroom, the older man took the opportunity to introduce himself to her. Even though she wasn't interested in him, she was flattered by the attention and didn't know how to extricate herself. Without thinking, she told him her first *and* last name and the name of the company where she worked. Those actions alone gave him a signal that she might be interested. The next day, he called her, saying he got her number from directory assistance. When she didn't return his call, he e-mailed her, figuring out her address from her company Web site. Bottom line: You need to be strategic in putting your Cablight on, or turning it off.

Other ways you can have your Cablight on too bright include staring too hard at someone, which can come across as stalker-ish, or asking him out instead of waiting for him to ask you, which comes across as controlling.

It's also on too bright if you're just "on" without targeting specific guys. If you're trying to get attention indiscriminately, you're not being strategic. Dancing on the bar will get you attention from all over the place, but you're much better off just trying to catch the eye of one or two guys you find attractive and/or intriguing. (When you're done dancing on the bar, of course.) No guy wants to date a girl who seems like she wants to be the center of everybody's universe—just his. The goal isn't for every guy to get your phone number. Just the right guy. Like I always say, "You're only looking for one."

OFF-DUTY SIGN

Oops. Are you doing things that might give the impression that you're not available? Maybe you wear a ring on your left ring finger, figuring that you just like it and that guys don't notice wedding rings much. Guess what? They do. Or when you go out somewhere to read in order to maybe attract some attention, are you so engrossed in your book that you wouldn't even notice if Matthew McConaughey sat down right next to you? Maybe you always answer "How are you?" with a negative response, like "I'm tired." Way to put a halt to a potential conversation! Another common mistake is taking yourself out of a conversation

---

Advice from Dan Aferiat,
Your On-Call Therapist

Should you be active or passive in the dating process?

Take along an "active" attitude everywhere you go. Be nonjudgmental, open, and courageous. Allow yourself many opportunities to make mistakes. Try to evaluate yourself based not on results (number of dates), but on your shift in attitude and behavior. For example, if you're trying go out and get dates, but you're not getting immediate results, give yourself some credit for the fact that you are making an effort. At the same time, be passive by trying to let yourself be upset and emotional when things don't work out. Let yourself sit with those feelings. Sadness, hurt, and anger are often difficult emotions to tolerate, so you need to be a good friend to yourself.

with multiple people because you decide you have nothing left to contribute. So, think of something. Or change the subject.

SELECTIVE SHYNESS

Some of my clients will tell me that they think they have their Cablights on, only they seem to be attracting the wrong people: like the cafeteria guy or their bus driver. The reason why is that it's easy to be friendly to them—you have nothing to lose. But if it's a guy you like, you're too shy to show you're interested. Women are often overly polite to people like doormen and taxi drivers because they feel uncomfortable having someone do a service for them; on the flip side, it's even more uncomfortable smiling at a guy for no reason. Try to examine who you're shining your light for, and more important, who's not getting beamed because you're worried he won't respond. You might not be aiming high enough, out of fear of rejection. Next time you see a guy you're tempted to shy away from, turn that Cablight *on!* You know those diva chicks who have a sense of entitlement, thinking every guy MUST like them? Be like that. Make yourself believe that you're a hot babe they want to get to know. Fake it until you make it, if you have to. Remember "The Party That Is You" and make it "The Bash of the Century"!

4

The 15-Hour Breakdown

You may think I'm asking too much of you by telling you to devote 15 hours a week to the search. But I've been at this awhile, and guess what? It works. If you're seriously committed to finding someone in the next 6 months, what's 15 hours a week anyway? Some of you probably already spend that much time commiserating with friends about not having a guy. So I'm giving you a proactive Plan to find one. Like I said before, if you had a boyfriend, you'd probably want to spend 15 hours a week with him, so why not spend the time looking for him? He's worth it. And your happiness is worth it.

DIVERSIFY!

The overall idea when spending 15 hours per week on your search for a guy is that you should diversify. Think of it as you would investing savings. You could put all your money into one stock and maybe do okay, but you'll be a much savvier investor if you spread your money between stocks, mutual funds, and some bonds and real estate. So get those thoughts of spending all 15 hours online out of your head right now. And, while it's fun to do your 15 hours with your girlfriends in tow, try to do some of this alone. Or at least have your own plan of where to go with friends, so you're not just tagging along wherever they go. As you'll soon realize, it's crucial to the process to take charge. Following are a few ideas.

Classes

This can be a great way to meet a guy. But you need to be sure to take something guy-friendly, like real estate investment or beer-making, not pottery or knitting. Keep your age and goals in mind, too. One client of mine took an acting class, and it was filled with twenty-year-olds who were actually looking at acting as a career, not a lark.

Singles Events

There are lots of activities in every city, organized specifically for singles. It can be a wine tasting or maybe some disco bowling, or just a regular happy-hour scene. You might think everyone who goes to these events is desperate, but not so. You might even meet a cool chick on the same quest you are.

> **In My Clients' Words**
>
> *I went to my first 8MinuteDating event the other night and my first thought was: "Attack of the Bland Businessmen." But I tried to keep an open mind, and I did end up meeting some interesting people. I'd definitely go back, because even though I didn't meet anyone I felt a connection with that night, I had fun! —Robin*

Bars

You might like the idea of going to a bar because you think the guys will be of a higher caliber than the guys at singles events.

But you need to look carefully because there's also going to be a much higher percentage of guys who are more into sex than relationships. Make sure you pick a bar that's you. If you like guys who are into sports, try a sports bar (you don't have to pretend to be into sports yourself—just don't interrupt at key moments). If you like more sophisticated guys, try more loungy, expensive bars. Use your local bar guide or free weekly paper to find one that's you. Different bars have different age ranges, too. A lot of bar scenes tend to skew young. One client of mine likes European men, so she goes to "French Tuesdays" at a bar near her. Also, don't barhop. If a place is completely dead, move to another. But don't switch up every round. You never know when some guy might be waiting for his opportunity to approach you. How can he if you disappear? And you never know who might walk in five minutes after you've left. Remember, you're only looking for one. Staying put makes it much more likely that you will meet that one.

> *Anthropologists have found that people meet more easily at bars in places like L.A., where going to another bar means driving for half an hour, than in New York, where people don't drive, and so they barhop right down the street, missing opportunities.*
>
> **Fun Fact**

The Gym

The gym is a great place to meet guys. You can't count your regular workout toward the 15 hours, but if you hang out at the juice bar afterward (iPod *off!*) and attempt to meet men, that's great. Or take some extra time to learn a new machine and ask a guy near it to help you. Don't take it personally if he's preoccupied with his workout. (Guys can be very focused at the gym.) It's a total cliché, I know, but guys like helping girls with stuff, so you may as well use that to your advantage. Don't forget to introduce yourself, either. He'll be more likely to say hi the next time he sees you. In fact, this is very important no matter where you meet a guy. Get your name out there as soon as possible. Just a quick "By the way, I'm Jen," will do. No need to make a big production out of it. It will be a subtle way of telling him that you are interested. And don't hang around afterward trying to make conversation. Be respectful of his workout and let him make the next move. Now, if you're one of those women who says "Oh, I look awful at the gym . . . I could never flirt with anyone there," get over it! You look strong and cool and energized. What could be better? If you're too preoccupied with your makeup or hair, you're missing out on a lot. Remember: Your Cablight comes from within.

Networking Parties

Most industries have organizations that throw parties and events. Look on the Web or in trade publications and check with your colleagues. I'd say a good half of the people there have very little interest in shoptalk. They go there mostly to socialize. While there's no guarantee that some people won't be married (watch the left ring fingers), you will find a lot of single guys there. It shouldn't be at all hard to steer the conversation onto more personal than professional topics. If you're in a male-dominated field, definitely take advantage of that. Why pass up opportunities where the men are certain to outnumber the women? All eyes will be on you.

Religious Activities

If you're at all religious, you can get a lot more out of your place of worship than prayer meetings, masses, or synagogue services. There are often planned outings that you can try out. Even at the services themselves, you can often meet and mingle afterward. Do an occasional charity activity, too. (Yes, I'm telling you to use charity as a guise to meet men—it can be for *two* good causes.)

Organizational Events

You know those flyers you always ignore for poetry readings, art gallery talks, literary club meetings, political lectures? If you have even an iota of interest in the topic, just go. You'll share at least one common interest with everyone in attendance, and you might even enjoy yourself, too. One client of mine moved to the suburbs and had no idea where to meet men out there. Then she saw a flyer for the local golf association, realizing that there is an abundance of cute men on the golf course and not nearly as many women. Plus, women's golf clothes are very cute these days.

Online

While I don't want you spending all your time online, I do want you to spend about three hours over the course of the week. It's a great tool and, if done right, it will garner some quality dates for you. It's relatively efficient (considering that dating is an inefficient process by nature), and it's right at your fingertips. So why not? I'll go into more detail in chapter eight, but for now, just try to use your online time wisely. No spending hours IMing with guys you haven't met yet, for instance.

Your Network of Friends

Sit down and make a list of everyone you know. Even if you haven't talked to some of them in a while, take the opportunity to call them and ask them to set you up. The "six degrees of separation" law says that the guy out there for you probably knows *someone* that you know, even if it's a remote connection.

Public Places

This is often the most challenging, because it's harder to know who's single. You also may need to make the opening line more often than you might in other situations. But you're going to see that it can be extremely effective when mastered. It catches guys off-guard, and they like it. Go to your local hangout, a neighborhood bar, a Barnes & Noble, or a Starbucks and try to actually meet people. I'm not asking you to wear a name tag and buy rounds of coffee for everyone. Just turn on that Cablight and see if you can meet a few guys. Smile, engage with your eyes, ask him about the book he's reading.

Hot Spot	Cold Spot
Crunch	Curves
Baseball game	Stars on Ice
Car shows	Fashion shows
Driving range	Knitting circle
"Chillin' and Grillin'" class	French Desserts 101
Billiards bar	Manicure bar
Wall Street	Rodeo Drive
The Home Depot	Victoria's Secret

ATTENTION, KNOW-IT-ALLS

Now, you may think you know without a doubt that you're going to meet a guy through your friends and that's that, so why even bother spending time online or at singles events or the other places I'm suggesting you try? The reason is, you *don't* know. It very well could—and probably will—happen where you least expect it. When I had my dating café, Drip, I was single and thought I was definitely going to meet someone there. With constant access to thousands of single guys, why wouldn't I?! But I ended up meeting my husband on the street (well, outside of a party, but more on that later . . .). I didn't even want to go out that night. I had to get out of my comfort zone. My friend stood me up, and I had to go alone. You just never know. So don't put all your eggs in one basket. You can't control exactly how it will happen.

A woman who attended one of my seminars made a point of e-mailing me to say she disagreed with my telling the women in attendance that they should try new things, like going to a bar alone. Her point was that she was an outdoorsy type who was far more likely to meet a guy on a Sierra Club outing than at a smoky bar. A few weeks later, she wrote again to say that one night after a singles event, she decided to try going to a bar alone after all, and she met a great guy whom she started dating. A few months after that, she wrote to say they'd become engaged!

So be open to trying new things. Be open to doing things alone. You might think it's smart and decidedly more fun to go out with your best girlfriend, but if you never meet anyone when you're with her, then . . . time for a new plan, right? You can't have preconceived notions of what will and won't work. It could even happen when you're running out for coffee in sneakers and sweats with no makeup on. Sometimes your Cablight is even brighter then because you're not putting on such an act and you don't care so much. It makes you more vulnerable and approachable, and more yourself.

GOING OUT ALONE

Some of my clients are deathly afraid of going out alone when I first meet with them. They say they could never do it and how

---

Advice from Dan Aferiat,
Your On-Call Therapist

How can you deal with your fears of trying something new?

You have to be willing to stretch yourself and anticipate that there will be a learning curve as you are challenged beyond the familiar. Anticipating change will be self-protective, as you begin to prepare yourself mentally, just as athletes do before sports events. Athletes prepare not just by knowing the game and their strategy, but also by knowing how to handle their emotions throughout the game. If you tell yourself that there will be some painful, confusing, and scary moments, it can help you to reformulate what the experience should be like, so that you can stay in the game. If you believe that relationships should be like being in calm water all the time, then any slight ripple, even in the early dating stages, will translate into fear. Alternatively, if you believe that relationships can be like oceans, where some days are peaceful and calm while other days have powerful riptides, you will be better equipped to handle the waves.

can I even ask such a thing? I ask them to do it because it works. You're not going to look like a loser or a freak or anything else you might be afraid of. I'm not asking you to go to a hopping club on a Saturday night with nothing but your tail between your legs to keep you company. (Although one client of mine went to a trendy New York City club alone after getting canceled on by a friend, and now she's good pals with the owner and gets VIP treatment there!) If you're not that daring, find a low-key but steadily busy bar in your neighborhood on a weeknight. Go with a girlfriend first, scope the place out, then brave it alone the next time. We've all seen a single woman reading at a bar or having some fries, chit-chatting with the bartender and enjoying herself. Do you honestly look at her and think she's a big loser? Hell no. You probably think she must be pretty darn cool. Guess what? So does every guy who walks through the door. And they want to know who she is!

If you've had to go out alone while traveling on business, you know it's really not that bad. You might think it's a lot different because it's another city and not one where you might run into someone you know, but hey, if that's the mental block, then pretend you're in Paris. You can bring a prop, or a magazine that you're not going to pay too much attention to. Maybe a crossword puzzle or a journal. Go to a restaurant bar at first if you think that might be less intimidating. Eat a yummy appetizer, have a glass of wine. I promise that if you do it just once, you'll get over your fears. It's one of those things you build up in your head to be really awful, kind of like escargot. Then it ends up not being so bad after all.

Now, when you do get approached by a guy, he may ask you why you're alone. Don't shy away! That's the best opening line he has, so answer. Tell him you wanted to get out of your apartment, you were craving a glass of merlot, or you can't resist the bar fries. It doesn't matter. Honestly? He doesn't care. He's just happy you *are* alone because it's about a thousand times easier to approach a woman alone than it is to approach two girlfriends who are engrossed in conversation.

DON'T THINK, JUST DO

When I first started my job as a headhunter, I used to overanalyze what would be the best move after every call. Should I fax the résumé now and call the manager back later? Or call now and fax later? Or wait five minutes and then call? My boss said to me: "Don't think, just do." I advise you to do the same in this Program. Don't keep getting ready to put yourself

> **In My Clients' Words**
>
> *When you're alone and you're female and you're fairly decent looking, you're literally a sitting duck. It's amazing how many people you can meet in one night, as long as you can disengage from the ones you're not interested in quickly enough. —Alev*

out there—just do it! Don't spend too much time worrying about how to handle it exactly right. The worrying is just an excuse to procrastinate doing something that is scary. It will never be perfect. Just get out there and do your 15 hours. You will make mistakes, but you will generate so many more dates in the process that it won't matter. You may find that the paths that you thought were dead ends might lead to something you didn't expect. And instead of spending all your time complaining about why you can't get a man and trying to strategize with all your friends, you'll be out there getting one.

STICK TO IT!

When you make a commitment for your 15 hours, you need to keep it. Plan out the following week every Sunday and keep those dates with yourself the same way you would with a friend. No canceling! The only time you're going to cancel is if you're asked out on a real date for that same block of time. Then you can reschedule whatever you were going to do toward your 15 hours that night. And no—a date does not count as part of the 15 hours. That's your reward for putting in that time. Some of my clients also ask if they should do more than 15 hours if they can, and I tell them not to. You need a couple of nights to yourself, away from the search. 15 hours is just enough.

OTHER OPPORTUNITIES

You just never know when and how he's going to come along. So activities you've said "no way" to in the past, I want you to start saying "sure" to now. I know you might be tired when your friend invites you to a party and it's way out of your way or you don't think you'll meet anyone there. Just push yourself to go. If you're worried you won't know anyone there, that's a good thing! Seek these opportunities out. A party is a great place to meet a guy. It's a bunch of people (who presumably have something in common) in an enclosed space with alcohol and music—what could be better?

Take the opportunity to get to know your city better, too. Go to art gallery events, meet-the-author sessions at your local bookstore (just try to pick a book guys would be interested in—not *Crocheting for Dummies*), learn how to rock climb at the local Y. Just because your sole intent is to meet a guy doesn't mean that's got to be the sole benefit (but it should be the main priority). Join a coed volleyball league or take some group tennis lessons. Instead of your girly candlelight yoga class at the gym, try a boxing class or martial arts, or something else more guy-friendly. Taking an interest in guy-friendly activities will also help you understand the male mentality.

MORE ON SETUPS

Don't use the excuse "My friends all know I'm single so they would set me up if they knew anyone." It's not always going to be your friends' first priority to be your personal matchmaker. Often, friends don't know that you want to be set up, and they are wrapped up in their own lives. But if you gently ask them to make it their agenda, they may think of someone that never occurred to them before. Tell them that you read this book and you are doing your homework and need their help. You have to work your network. You know the old adage—"You don't ask, you don't get." And the more you ask, the more they'll remember you the next time, even if they can't think of anyone right now. Hit up your married guy friends, too. Usually they won't want to get involved, but if you remind them, they will. You don't want to kick yourself for not trying.

Say yes to everything when it comes to setups. Have you always shied away from guys your mom has brought up? Maybe she really does know better than you. Or at least she could get lucky sometimes. You don't have to go out with him more than once, but be open and positive and grateful, and the next guy could be gold. Sure, sometimes you have to deal with nosy questions afterward when someone sets you up, but that just might be part of the bargain with certain people. They're doing you a favor, so just play along. Besides, just because they ask you to

Sample Week

Monday—One hour online to narrow down responses and pick three guys to initiate contact with myself. One hour at Starbucks, sitting in prominent chair, making eye contact. Talk to at least one guy.

Tuesday—One hour of coed volleyball at the gym. One hour at juice bar afterward. Attempt to talk to at least two guys.

Wednesday—One hour online. Respond to e-mails and set up possible dates.

Thursday—Two-hour Biotech Stock Basics class at city college. Talk to one guy before, one guy on break, one guy at the end. One hour alone time after at nearby bar. Bring textbook to see if anyone asks about it!

Friday—Three hours out with the girls to that bar that all those traders hang out at after work.

Saturday—Two hours at driving range. Try to get some help with swing from nearby guys. Two hours with Susie at sports bar to watch game. (Pay very little attention to Susie!)

Sunday—Date with Joe!

kiss and tell doesn't mean you can't be coy! You often hear stories about people turning down a blind date and then they end up meeting and marrying the exact same person three years later. Why make things so difficult for fate? You don't want to waste the chance to spend the rest of your life with the right guy just because you don't want to spend a mere hour with a few wrong ones. Plus, if you say yes to whomever your friend chooses, she will be likely to set you up again. If you act too picky, she might just give up.

Some people ask me about professional matchmakers, to which I say "Sure!" Give it a shot if you have the money and a good recommendation. However, you are not to count his or her efforts in finding you a match toward your 15 hours. They can't do the time for you.

OTHER THINGS THAT DON'T COUNT

- *Girl time.* If you sit and talk with your friend the whole night, it doesn't matter how hot you look or how hoppin' the bar is. If you're engrossed in a conversation with her, guys are not going to approach you, rendering your efforts useless. Spend your time wisely.

- *Your travel time.* I want you to eye guys on the subway, of course, but c'mon, your daily commute doesn't count, unless you strike up conversation along the way.

- *Any time at work.* I don't care how hard you're ogling that guy in accounting. Unless you do something about it, of course.

- *Dates.* As mentioned, the point is meeting new guys, not ones who have already asked you out. You have to keep up the 15 hours in order to line up a date for the next week. There's no guarantee that the date you are on will lead to a second date, even though the hope is that it will.

- *Going out with a dimmed Cablight.* If you go to Barnes & Noble but don't bother looking up from your magazine,

My 15 Hours Use this to plan out your first week. Try to put the 15 hours into your calendar each week, so that you make the commitment to yourself.	MON
TUE	**WED**
THU	**FRI**
SAT	**SUN**

you're doing a half-assed job of your 15 hours. It's not just about going out. It's about being on!

- *Being a wallflower.* There's no point in going to a singles event or a bar or anywhere else if you're going to stand in the corner looking like you don't want to meet anyone.

- *Your workouts.* If you're too into the zone and not zooming in on any guys, your workout doesn't count. It's fine for your treadmill time, but if you'd like to count any of your gym time toward your 15 hours, you need to smile at guys and not look like you're training for Beijing 2008. Or ask someone to spot you on the bench press.

5

It Happens When You **ARE** Looking

So, let me guess . . . you've been told countless times that "it always happens when you're not looking." You hear stories about how as soon as so-and-so threw in the dating towel and was resigned to the fact that she might be single forever, then *Bam!* the perfect guy appeared. Stories like these are misleading. They make it sound like it comes easily, without struggle. First of all, when I was single, I was always looking! I don't care how cynical, how "over it" any of these women say they were when they were magically discovered by Mr. Right; I'm not quite buying it. Hindsight is twenty-twenty. Perhaps they did hit rock bottom and had a realization that it might not happen for them. But they didn't give up. What usually happens in these cases is the woman starts to have a new outlook on dating: If it happens, great; if it doesn't, I'll deal with it. Instead of being controlling and trying to force relationships, she develops a confident, non-desperate attitude because she's not in such a panic anymore. When you're not panicked, your Cablight can really shine.

COURTSHIP RITUALS

Some women wonder why they have to try to meet a guy at all. They don't want to have to date to find one; they think something will develop within their group of friends or with someone at work (i.e., "the natural way"). But what happens in situations like these is you'll often flirt and flirt and never figure out if he's interested or not. Or you might even hook up with him one night and think, "Gee, we've been friends for so long . . . how perfect!" But you can't go into a relationship backward. Making out or even having sex does not change a relationship in a man's eyes if you haven't been leading toward that in a more formal manner. There are exceptions, of course, but it's a huge risk to bet the bank on getting a boyfriend this way.

Part of adopting a winning strategy in dating is knowing that there's an unspoken language or code that helps men and women communicate in the early stages of dating. There is so much that's unpredictable at the beginning of a relationship that there's a security in knowing that certain things are going to happen in a particular sequence (for instance: phone call leads to first date, first date leads to more dates, more dates lead to sex, etc.). It helps us make sense of one another. That said, you don't have to be a prude and take things to the extreme as though you're a relic from the 1950s.

You need the courtship ritual to give yourself some negotiating power in dating and to give him some guidance. Guys will often go for the easy friendship and/or the sex. They won't tend to spend money on you or call you if they don't have to, and they're happiest on the path of least resistance. If you're already in a friendship with this person or hooking up with him, you can't say, "How come you never take me out to a nice dinner?"

You have no bargaining position at that point because you have set a precedent. Go out and get yourself some good old-fashioned dates with boundaries and formalities and all that other seemingly stodgy stuff and you'll soon see why those things work to your advantage. I have found that there is a very specific courtship pattern that almost always leads to a lasting relationship. If you can navigate your dating strategy to follow courtship rituals, you greatly increase your relationship odds. More on this in chapter seven.

OBSTACLES

If you're still finding it very difficult to imagine spending 15 hours a week on your search, there may be some conflicts in your life that are going to interfere not only with your plans to find a guy, but also with your ability to make a commitment to one. I ask the women who come to me for coaching how they expect to have time for a relationship if they don't have 15 hours per week for the search. They always say to me, "If I were in a relationship, I'd make the time!" But it doesn't work that way. You need to make room in your life for a relationship to happen. Go back to thinking about your priorities. Is a relationship really something you want? If so, there are some things you may have to drop in order to find one.

The Ex

Even if he's not in your physical life anymore, he could be in your mental life. If you're looking back on the relationship with rose-colored glasses and you're still interested in what he's doing, who he's seeing, and whether he thinks about you as much as you do about him, that's a problem. Take a night off from driving past his house to see if his lights are on and think about the bad parts of the relationship. There is a reason you broke up! Do you honestly miss him or do you miss having him around? A guy way better for you is out there waiting—don't you want to find him? If you're still seeing your ex, that's an even bigger problem. Maybe you just hook up when he comes into town or you have phone sex here and there. Or maybe you're trying to be "friends." But if all your signals are directed toward him, you can't have your Cablight on for other guys. This is still too much like a relationship to let you whole-heartedly enter another. Keep in mind the mantra "Don't think, just do." And get back out there! No wallowing.

The Noncommittal Boyfriend

A lot of women will stay with someone who doesn't give them what they want because they have low self-esteem, or they think that there's no one better out there. Raise your standards. Dump the guy once and for all, since clearly he doesn't really want you or you don't really want him. Why are you wasting your time? Some women will say it's easier to meet someone while you're with someone else, but I've found that very rarely works out. Having a relationship on the back burner is going to cloud and complicate any new relationship you try to pursue. Odds are you're just trying to meet someone new to make boyfriend #1 jealous or you're going to compare #2 to #1 and not judge him on his own merit. Or you don't truly have your Cablight on.

A Hopeless Crush

A crush that's so intense you compare everyone to him can easily prevent you from going out and finding someone else. If you've tried to pursue something with the guy and it's not going anywhere, you need to let it go. Mourn the loss and move on, because if you try to go out while your thoughts are on him 24-7, you'll be disappointed in everyone you meet. A crush is an idealized view of a person, and comparing everyone to some false sense of perfection is not fair. You need to be free and clear of baggage like this, otherwise it's really going to hold you back in this Program. If, on the other hand, you have yet to see if this crush could be requited, now is the time. Carpe diem.

Your Job

Yes, I'm going to say it: If your job is going to get in the way of your 15-hour plan, either through too much travel or too many late hours, you might want to rethink whether you're truly ready for a relationship. If you decide a relationship is more important to you, you may have to make some changes in your life to accommodate one. Think about what I said about what's urgent and what's important. Getting that project in on time is more urgent, but taking steps to improve your lovelife is more important. Don't always choose work out of loyalty, and don't mistake your job for being more important than it is. Are you really going to get fired if you lighten your workload a little? You might not get promoted as fast, but is that what's going to make you happy ultimately? Look at your age and your stage in life and then see if you can afford the "luxury" of working like a slave, or if you've reached a point where your personal life is more important. You may even consider changing jobs. I'm not saying it's wrong to be into your career. But you may need to make choices and set priorities. If you travel two weeks per month, it's not that likely that you will find a relationship. If getting into a relationship is truly your Number One priority, you may have to change your schedule to reflect that.

One client of mine is in her early thirties and works in investment banking. She went to an Ivy League school and is incredibly smart and successful. But she decided a couple of years ago to derail from the vice-president track. Why? Because, while her job is important to her, she wanted time for her personal life. The risk of "waking up at forty and being miserable" because her job was all she had going for her was not one she wanted to take. Now she has time outside of work to make room for pursuing a great guy—that's something important to her that she was willing to put first.

A Friend Who Takes Up All Your Time

If you have a best friend, it can sometimes take the form of a surrogate relationship. Some girls are together so often and act so close, giggling and whispering and paying attention to nothing around them, guys probably assume they're lovers (and not in the hot "Can I join in?" kind of way). Complaining to and confiding in her could be wasting valuable time, too. Keep in mind that misery loves company; hanging out with her may be keeping you down. Spend less time with your girlfriend and more time trying to find a boyfriend. Set boundaries with her so that you can get what you want. In most cases, you don't need to go so far as to dump her. Just pull back. Start spending more time on your own while still having a fun evening with her once a week or however often you have time for outside of your 15 hours. If you decide to tell her that you're doing this Program and she decides she wants to join in, it's still important that you do much of your 15 hours on your own. As I explained, it doesn't work nearly as effectively when you're always with a friend, especially when it's the same friend.

Some girlfriends could intentionally be holding you back in dating, whether it's because they want to keep you all for themselves, or they're jealous of the attention you're getting. One of the women I coach always went out with the same friend to meet guys, but she started to notice that if a guy was interested in her, her "friend" would often try to move in on her territory (when guys do this to other guys, it's called "cock-blocking"!). One night, my client returned from the restroom only to find her dear friend kissing the guy she had just been flirting with for an hour. After that, she gave her the flick, realizing her "dating buddy" was causing her more harm than good.

CRITICAL MASS THEORY

You might think that this 15 hours thing will never work because you spend three hours now on searching for a guy and that's not leading to much of anything. It doesn't work that way. You need to make enough contacts to breed other opportunities. When you put in the 15 hours, you start to get on a roll. Sud-

> *Pick up Malcolm Gladwell's* The Tipping Point: How Little Things Can Make a Big Difference *to understand more about the critical mass concept.*
>
> Quick Tip

denly, it's raining men! A lot of single women will describe their dating lives as coming in waves. They'll go through a dry spell, then they'll have a really busy spell. It all depends on how much energy you're putting out.

One client of mine cut her hours from 15 to around half of that, because she simply didn't want to devote so much time to her search, and she got no dates during that period. She went back to doing her full 15 hours shortly after. She admitted that in order to really reap in the success, she had to put in the time.

POSITIONING

Your main goal in trying to get a guy to come your way is to make it easy for him. So if you're stuck in a corner with your girlfriends, get up and hit the jukebox or watch a game of pool. Go to the bar when you see him go for a drink, even if it's just to order water. Position yourself in a place where he can easily approach you. If you're near his table at a Starbucks, drop your pen or magazine, so he at least looks up. (Hopefully he'll pick it up for you!) And when you do get into a conversation with him, turn your body toward him. It sounds basic, I know, but some women think it's better to be cool and to turn away. Sure it's cool, but it's not very effective in getting dates. You have to do the opposite of "turning the cold shoulder."

One of the women I coach went to a dinner party with arranged seating and noticed that she was grouped with two girls, when what she really wanted was to sit next to a cute guy she'd eyed there. So she pulled her friend aside and asked if she could switch the place cards. The friend was a little annoyed, but what's more important? Your own happiness or a friend being mildly irked? Instead of being miserable, gazing at the guy from afar all through dinner, she got to flirt with him one-on-one.

OPENING LINES

So, what if the guy you've been eyeing doesn't catch on that you'd love for him to talk to you? You might have to take matters into your own hands by being the first person to say something. Remember, you're not going to ask him out. You're just opening a window for him to meet you. Don't worry if it doesn't

---

Top Ten Women's Opening Lines

10. "How are the margaritas here?"
9. "Do you have the time?"
8. "You look familiar."
7. "Do you live around here? I was wondering if you knew of a good bookstore nearby."
6. "This cell phone is new—can you figure out how to change the ring tone?"
5. "Have you been here before?" (Contrary to popular belief, this isn't a cheesy pickup line if asked sincerely.)
4. "Is that a good book? I'm looking for something great to read."
3. "If you're done with it, do you think I could check out the arts section of your paper?"
2. "Would you mind watching my stuff while I grab another coffee?"
1. "Hi."

---

sound original. If it starts a conversation, it doesn't matter what was said or who spoke first!

Now, just because you have the opening line doesn't mean you're in the male role. He's going to lead from here. You simply put it out there and then let him take the lead. But you may have to keep your Cablight on "bright" so he knows you're interested in more than the time. Don't give up after your initial question. Sometimes he'll be wildly attracted to you within five seconds, but that's rare. If you don't happen to look like Gisele Bündchen (and most of us don't), you might have to push the conversation slightly longer than is comfortable in order to get his attention. Try to get your name in there early on. It breaks the ice. "By the way, I'm Sarah," shows that you'd like to get to know him better, in a nonthreatening, nonaggressive way.

Don't worry about saying something stupid. If you saw *Dirty Dancing*, you probably recall the scene where Jennifer Grey's character, Baby, met Patrick Swayze's Johnny at that party. The first thing he heard her say was "I carried a watermelon." She was mortified, but he didn't care what she had said. And Baby gets the guy! Remember: The guy doesn't really notice what you're saying, he's just going to know you talked to him.

There was a great scene on *Felicity* once where Felicity's friend Noel had developed a huge crush on her. They're playing Scrabble, and she is talking to him. He's supposed to be listening to her talking, but he just tunes her out like Charlie Brown's teacher at one point because he's so distracted by her in every other way. He's looking into her eyes, seeing her hair and her face, and her words are a blur. This isn't a bad thing! Women always complain about men not listening to them, but in some cases, it can actually be a good sign, because you've put him in la-la land.

> **In My Clients' Words**
>
> *From the female end, I've noticed that a little can go a long way when it comes to being the first to talk. I was at a bar once and this guy came in, looked around, left, then came back in, so I just said to him "Are you confused?" It was that easy. He sat down next to me and we ended up dating for a few months. —Tina*

If you sense that there is a spark between you as you're talking, try to give him openings that will lead to him asking you out. When you're at a bar, it's a given that people are there to socialize and meet potential dates. But if you're at a business conference or at a coffee shop and you've struck up a conversation with a guy, you might have to move the conversation to subjects that are a little more personal or even sexy. That way, it doesn't just seem like you're networking or into talking to strangers.

You don't need to segue into a conversation about pole dancing (bravo if you can). Just guide the conversation to anything personal in nature: vacations, favorite restaurants, weekend plans. If you can somehow work into the conversation the fact that you're single—by saying you live alone, so it's nice to get out and meet new people, or that you have to do your laundry this weekend, or anything along those lines—you're giving him a clue that you're available and possibly interested. If nothing I've mentioned seems natural to bring up, try sports, music, or even your favorite TV shows. Anything that can give you some common ground to initiate a spark. Talking about work, or worse yet, grilling him about his work, will make the conversation feel more like a job interview than flirting.

> *A study on flirting by the Social Issues Research Centre in Oxford, England, found: "When you first meet new people, their initial impression of you will be based 55% on your appearance and body language, 38% on your style of speaking and only 7% on what you actually say."*
>
> **Quick Tip**

Your body language should be saying something, as well. Position yourself toward him, the way I told you. Also think of how animals have their mating rituals. They don't talk, but there's no mistaking what's going on when a female is strutting around and a male is circling her. This is body language extreme, but you can also fluff your feathers a little or shake your mane to let him know you're interested. This is going to have a much stronger effect on a guy than anything you might say. Another winning move: If you're in a place that has music, sway to it, dance in place a little. Show the open and sexy side of your personality.

THE ART OF REJECTION

In order to maximize your 15 hours, you don't want to waste time on people you know you're not interested in. I might count the three hours you spent stuck talking with the loser guy in the corner one week, but I'm not going to count it the next! Of course you don't want to be rude, but there are a number of ways to get out of a conversation. The most effective is usually to start with, "Well, it was really nice to meet you, but . . ." and then just pick an excuse: I'd better get back to my friends/I've got to go to the ladies' room/I'm going to go get a drink/I think I see someone I know . . . Or even give no excuse at all. Just say "Well, it was really nice to meet you," and move on.

The key is in the tone. It has to be friendly but firm, so you're saying no in an effective way, not one that's going to encourage him to try harder or follow you. Pretend you're a gorgeous movie star trying to brush off a fan; she'd be super nice, but you

Learning to say no to guys has saved me so much wasted time. It's also helped in my relationships with other people. I bought a car recently and my dad, who thinks I spend too much money, asked me, "So how much did that cost you?" And I answered back, "It cost none-of-your-business." He actually complimented me and said I handled that really well with him!
—Kathy

know she wouldn't let him think she wanted to talk to him again. You can also use your body to reject people, by the way. If you turn away while saying, "Well, it was nice to meet you," he's going to turn away, too. People

If you're hiring someone for a job, you wouldn't want to discriminate based on race, religion, age, hairline, or otherwise, but in dating, you are supposed to have your preferences. That's what dating is all about!

Quick Tip

are so worried about hurting someone's feelings. Have some sympathy for yourself and your own feelings. Your time is valuable. Your job is not to make some guy feel better. You can be polite and still take care of yourself.

If you find that you're always the girl that the loser guy corners, or you always get stuck talking to the hot guy's loser friend, you're way too nice. Some people in this situation secretly like the attention, though. They may think they hate rejecting people, but they hate *being* rejected even more, so getting "stuck" with the loser guy is a way to play it safe. Examine what's really going through your head when you're not walking away from those situations faster. Push yourself to aim a little higher. Don't take rejecting so seriously, either. It's not a mortal wound you're inflicting on him—he'll live. Just don't drag it out. Ultimately, you'll hurt him more if you talk to him for two hours and then give him a fake phone number than if you give him the slip within the first five minutes.

LEAVE HIM WANTING MORE

A lot of people ask me how to end conversations with guys they do like. This is an important question because you really don't

Advice from Dan Aferiat, Your On-Call Therapist

If you don't seem to like anyone—what does that mean?

The goal that one aims for when first meeting someone new is to reach a point where you believe you have enough information about the other person to accept or reject them. Uncertainty is normal in dating as you begin to develop a sense of who that person really is beyond your fantasy, and whether there is a "fit." Generally, in your conscious mind, you'll shift back and forth between thinking positive and negative things about a guy, which can be very confusing. Furthermore, your unconscious contributes to this process. If you find yourself repeatedly and suddenly downgrading men after liking them initially, it suggests that you are trying to protect yourself. If the conscious thought is that "he is not man enough," perhaps the unconscious thought is that "you are not woman enough." The more useful approach is to be aware of your uncertainty and use that awareness to slow yourself down and be curious about who this person really is.

need to talk to a guy all night in order to see him again. You can, but it should be able to work for you either way. If you are really connecting, keep it going until you have to leave and end it then. The best way to end it is in a friendly, flirty, and very reluctant manner, with a splash of dare thrown in. It's like a game of tag where you're trying to get him to chase you. Smile, maybe cock your head a little, and say, "Well, it was nice to meet you . . ." but this time you should hold eye contact for a while and see what he does. You are giving him his cue and leading him to ask for your number. Note that this is very different from the "It was nice meeting you" blow-off line. The trick is in the flirting and the body language. If you are using all your charm and flirting tactics, and he doesn't ask for your number, walk away. At that point, once you've shown interest, you need to let him chase you.

WHEN HE REJECTS YOU

Yes, it hurts. How dare he not like you?! But you need to accept it and move on. It's nothing personal. You just weren't the piece for his puzzle. Try to think of it as him doing you a favor by realizing it first. Would you rather date him for months and then have him tell you? Some people click with you, some people don't. That's just dating. So don't blame yourself or think that every guy isn't going to like you, and don't immediately assume you did something wrong. Sometimes, it's just not a fit. The only time you should look at what you did is if the same thing is happening over and over in the same way. If there's a pattern, then you should look at your actions. If you never get asked for your number, or if all your first dates end abruptly, see if you're doing anything that might be considered controlling, clingy, judgmental, or otherwise unattractive. And keep reading for ways to break the pattern.

Whatever you do, don't put yourself down after he's let you down. It's not healthy to think "I'm not pretty enough" or "He must only like skinny girls." If you're going to make up reasons, use ones that protect your ego. Laugh it off and move on. Back when I was single and just learning about dating (I was about twenty-two), I met a guy I liked, and things were moving along well, getting toward "relationship status." He said he had to go on a trip to Florida, and that he'd call when he got back. I

Top Five Excuses for Him Not Liking You

5. He must be intimidated by my beauty and/or success.
4. He's not mature enough for me anyway. He probably still lives with his mother.
3. He's got serious issues. It's going to take years of therapy before he's ready for a relationship.
2. I'm a Democrat, he's a Republican . . . it never would have worked anyway.
1. He's totally gay!

---

waited and waited. I never heard from him again. Of course it's clear that he didn't want to keep dating me, but I still call him "the guy who went to Florida and never came back!"

WING WOMEN

The reason why I discourage you from going out with a girlfriend to do your 15 hours is not because I don't think you should be surrounded by supportive, encouraging friends, but because often they can get in your way when you're trying to meet guys. If you do feel strength in numbers, keep in mind that it's better to go out in groups of three or more than one-on-one, because if a guy does want to talk to you and you feel like you can't leave your friend alone for more than five minutes, that's going to hold you back. Still, if you do have a friend who's outgoing, understands the process, isn't competitive, and is also looking for a guy, then you might be able to help each other. Just make sure you don't play second fiddle to her and that you aren't afraid to compete with her for guys. All's fair in love and war. Try to determine which of your friends you have the most success with, too. For instance, "When I go out with Maria, I always meet great guys,

I finally found a great dating buddy. We like going to the same kinds of places, we like completely different types of guys, and she's okay being left alone if I start talking to someone. We don't get in each other's way, but we're also really supportive of each other. —Sara

but when I go out with Kate, all she does is whine." I always say, "Don't argue with what works." Watch the patterns. If Maria is good luck, make her your new wing woman!

YOUR DATING MENTORS

You can also have dating buddies who don't go out with you. If you have an already-attached friend who really got it right when she was dating, you can take advice from her. Don't abuse the privilege, though. She's not your dating coach. (You have to pay for those.) Try to take advice only from those who have worked things out well for themselves. If you have a married friend whose marriage you wouldn't want, then don't take her advice. People often want you to be like them and have what they have. As such, don't take advice from your single friends, either.

One thing I also want to warn against is relying on your mother for advice. There are a lot of women in their twenties and thirties who still talk to their mothers about every detail in their dating lives. You often can't please your mother and yourself at the same time. Your mom might want you to marry someone who meets her criteria, when those qualities aren't important to you. Or she might think no one's good enough for you, so she'll come up with reasons why you should drive everyone away. She usually does have good intentions, but she doesn't have the answers, and she is biased. Women who are too close to their moms, in the sense that they share everything with them, are usually the least successful in dating. Despite your being raised to think so, Mother does not always know best. She's just another woman when it comes right down to it, and she's just as prone to giving bad advice as anyone else. Chances are, you might even see some of the mistakes that she has made in her own relationship(s). One client of mine was holding back in her dating life, partly because she saw how poorly her own parents got along and didn't want to go through the same thing in her own life. After working with me, she started to realize that her parents probably should have divorced years ago. It ended up being very liberating for her to acknowledge that her mother had made some choices that she wouldn't have made herself.

It also creates extra pressure on you if you have to answer to your mother about everything. You don't need to feel like you've let her down when something doesn't work out with a guy. Mothers are natural meddlers, too. If you're waiting for him to call and she knows it, do you really want *her* calling every ten minutes to ask if he has yet? Try to cut what you tell her in half and see what happens. When you're not using your mother or your friends as a crutch, you might find yourself a lot less crippled in dating than you thought. You will find that you have your own opinion, and this realization will make you impervious to their advice.

LEARNING TO JUGGLE

You know that saying, "When you assume, it makes an *ass* out of *u* and *me*"? Well, you're going to feel like a huge ass if you get too presumptuous. It's very important in this Program to have a lot of pots on the stove at once. If you meet someone and say, "I *know* he's the One for me!" and shut off all your dating channels and start turning guys down, you're doing yourself a disservice. You might be right, and that's the day you're hoping for, right? If you didn't believe you'd *know* one day, that would take a lot of the thrill out of looking for him. But we've all thought a guy was "the One" when he wasn't, so proceed with caution. Remember to keep your hopes high but your expectations low. When people say "You just know," they are always speaking with the benefit of hindsight. Unless he's brought up the idea of being exclusive, and you've been out with him a bunch of times and seen his pattern, don't assume anything. Keep on juggling and putting those feelers out there, 'cause you never know which one might pan out.

POSITIVE ATTITUDE!

You may find when you're doing your 15 hours that you miss the mark sometimes. Maybe the driving range sucks on Saturday mornings, or your local Starbucks happens to be frequented only by gay guys and senior citizens. Maybe the things you thought would work didn't, but odds are, a few things you didn't think would work, will. Switch your schedule around according to what seems to be working and what isn't. Try another Starbucks, or a weeknight at the driving range instead. The bottom line is that you have to put in the time and look everywhere for a while. Pay attention to what works, and follow the strategies that work best for you. Keep your Cablight on and be optimistic!

Which brings us back to that "It always happens when you're not looking" thing. . . . Another reason you might hear that from people you've sought advice from is that they are trying to lift your spirits. It's tough to see a friend struggling, so they want to tell you to leave it up to fate because fate always comes through. And you should definitely keep your faith! But I'm here to tell you that you've got to give fate a helping hand. If you look in the right way, it *will* happen. The how and the when might be out of your control, but if you have the right attitude and put in the time and effort, you *will* have success. Someday you'll be the married chick telling a single friend, "It happened when I *was* looking—because I finally learned how to look!"

6

Guy Translation

"There's a lotta things about me you don't know anything about, Dottie. Things you wouldn't understand. Things you couldn't understand." —PEE-WEE HERMAN IN PEE-WEE'S BIG ADVENTURE

*T*he biggest thing you need to know about men is that you should read their actions and not their words. Of course, it's natural to want to hear things like "Oh, you're the most beautiful woman in the world . . . I've never met anyone like you . . . You complete me. . . ." But how many guys really talk that way outside of a Cameron Crowe movie? They're usually a lot more subtle than we'd like them to be. But that's not to say you can't read them. While a guy may not be saying he wants to spend every waking moment with you until the end of eternity, if he's been consistent and reliable in asking you out, and has a very cute way of looking at you when you are on a date, these are pretty good signs. You may be tempted to ask what he's thinking, to force him to share every single emotion. Don't! Just relax and enjoy the moment. Often, he's feeling the same feelings you are, but he doesn't express them the same way. Even men who have been madly in love for fifty years aren't as effusive as their wives might like. Instead, he'll surprise her with an anniversary cruise, or pick up that bracelet she was eyeing, or he'll just re-member to take out the garbage each week because he knows it makes her happy.

The occasional man will talk a big game, saying you're the most wonderful woman in the world and that he can't wait to take you to Paris one day, but don't believe the hype. Wait to see what kind of man he is first, in his phone calls and his follow-through. This is not to say the guy's lying when he says those things. But it's often just as much a fantasy to him as it is to you. It's not reality until he actually does it. Some of my clients will get very excited after a date with a guy, saying, "He said we should go to a Broadway show next time!" That is not a

Empty Words vs.	Meaningful Action
He says he's going to take you to Paris someday.	He takes you out to a French bistro.
He says he wants you to bear his children.	He brings you over to meet his sister and her kids.
He says you make him forget all other women.	He stops dating other women.
He says he can't stop thinking about you.	He calls you.
He says all his friends would love you.	He introduces you to his friends.
He says you mean more to him than anything.	He skips his workout to go to your work event.
He says he can't wait to see you.	He plans a great date and shows up.

promise, I tell them. Until he actually calls and produces tickets to said event, just consider it a thought, not a plan. He meant it at the time, but this does not necessarily have any bearing on whether it will happen. He was living in the moment, and, as frustrating as that realization might be to a woman, living in the moment is something we can embrace ourselves.

THE GAME OF CHICKEN

Your actions count, too, and he's going to put a lot more stock into what you do than what you say. Often, women will play it cool on a date. It becomes a game of chicken, seeing who will give in first and admit they dig the other person. If you're lucky, the guy will let down his guard before you do by saying something like "You're really fun/nice/easy to talk to." After that, you feel like you can be more yourself, and the date will be much more productive as well as romantic. But make it your job to let down your guard first. You can do it just by looking up at him from your veal piccata with a little smile, or by being seductive with your eyes, alternating between looking at his lips and his eyes while he talks. The way that you show your interest is with your eyes, smile, body language, and by stroking his ego in a flirty way (without kissing up). If you don't take that role into your own hands by flirting with him and acting like you're interested, he's not going to have enough of a clue that you like him.

MEN HAVE "HIGHER STANDARDS"

While a woman should and will go out with a guy more than once even if she's not completely sure if she likes him or not, men aren't often willing to do that with women. The primary reason is that they're the ones who are usually paying! That may sound shallow or cheap, but ask yourself if you'd really fork over another $50 to $100 on someone you feel lukewarm about, or who might feel lukewarm about you. This is why it's crucial to really have your Cablight on during the first date. Do all you can to let him see that glow that he's bringing out in you, even if it's not a natural glow yet. (Your rosy cheeks aren't natural, either, but we all fake that.) If you don't, how is he going to know you'd like to go out again, even if you say you do? See, just as men prove themselves with actions rather than words, they're reading you in the same way. You can talk until you're blue in the face about how you'd like to see him again, but unless you're backing it up with some pretty strong body language and sex signals (using your eyes and lips, as I described in chapter three), he's not going to get that you mean it. If he says, "I would love to take you out again," and you give the stock answer of "Sure, that would be great," how will he know you're not just being polite? You'd say "sure" even if you weren't interested, and he knows that. So, the difference has to be in your tone, your facial expressions, and your body language. For a guy to ask you out on subsequent dates, he needs to feel like he's going to get somewhere with you physically. That doesn't mean immediately, but you need to at least give him hope for the future. If you're at all interested in him, even if you think he's probably not "the One," go for the kiss at the end if he leans in for one. See if there could be chemistry.

THE TENNIS GAME

United States Tennis Association RULE #21:
WHEN TO SERVE & RECEIVE. The server shall
not serve until the receiver is ready. However, the receiver

> *shall play to the reasonable pace of the server and*
> *shall be ready to receive within a reasonable time of the*
> *server being ready.*

A lot of my clients don't understand why it's better not to call a guy until he's called first. Think of it as a tennis game in which it's always his serve. You're meant to hit the ball back, and you can hit it back hard, but if you want to see what kind of man he is, you can't be the one making the moves. For instance, he may have said he wanted to go out with you again, but you beat him to the punch by being the one to call the next day. Now you'll never know how long it might have taken him to call on his own, or if he would have at all. Guys are often more easygoing than we are, so he very well might go out with you again just because you're asking and it's easy enough to go see a movie or grab a bite with someone (especially if you're also sharing the expense), but inevitably, you're going to get fed up with always playing the role of the pursuer. He's also likely, inevitably, to turn you down. If he didn't like you enough to call in the first place, he's generally not going to like you enough to stick around for long. Further, most guys feel more comfortable being "the man" (i.e., being the one leading). It makes them feel more confident and manly, which will in turn make them more attractive to you. Just as in ballroom dancing, the man leads, yet the woman is not passive. In terms of the tennis game, you can hit the ball back hard. How hard, you ask? Say it's your fourth date and he's called to ask you to go out to dinner— why not kick things up a notch and offer to cook dinner at your place instead? It makes for a more intimate date and moves the relationship forward a little, without you being pushy about it.

Although you should let the man take the lead in most cases, it is okay to make the very first move. You can send a flirty e-mail to a guy whose online profile interests you, or make small talk with the cute guy next to you at the bar without appearing overly forward. In fact, guys often need the encouragement to get the ball rolling. Keep it limited to one move, though. Remember that you don't want to make two moves in a row. Sit tight. You did the right thing by expressing your interest. But now it's his serve. It's important to see what kind of man he is, and you can do that by letting him take control. If he doesn't? You have your answer, even if it's not the one you were hoping for.

WHY MEN DON'T CALL WHEN THEY SAY THEY WILL

I get this question a lot, and there is an answer for it. Sometimes, they just consider it part of the protocol. It's polite to say "I'll call you," just as it would be to say "It was nice to meet you." It's a natural way to end a date. If he doesn't say it, it doesn't feel like a proper good-bye, and you both end up feeling awkward. However, sometimes men are trying to gauge your response, trying to gauge if you'd like them to call. So make sure your reaction is positive. If you say "I'd *really* like that" in a sexy voice while looking into his eyes, it's giving him a very different impression than if you say "Okay, great" with a cold handshake.

There are many reasons why a guy says he'll call and doesn't, even if you did all the right things. He might have had a super time with you, but the chemistry was more friendly than romantic. Or maybe you were a great diversion, but he's still hung up on his ex-girlfriend. It could also be that he didn't think you were as into him as he was into you. Men are just as afraid of rejection as we are.

You can't undo a negative impression you left on him the last time you saw him by calling him and expressing an interest the next day, either. All you would accomplish at that point is making him think you're pushy and controlling. Pick up and move on. And don't beat yourself up trying to think of things you might have done wrong on the date. Any one thing you do won't completely blow it. If it's really killing you that a week or two has gone by and you haven't heard from him

> *When a guy doesn't call, you might be tempted to think, "What's wrong with me?" and get depressed about it. But it's more truthful to realize: "He's not the guy I thought he might be. . . . So why do I care so much?" —Kim*

In My Clients' Words

and you think you might have had your Cablight off, you can try to call him. Be breezy, be light, and immediately let him take the lead again. It is a long shot, but it's worth it when you have nothing to lose. Just keep those hopes high and your expectations low and you'll be okay.

THE OVERDUE CALLER

There are some cases in which a guy will say he'll call you on Tuesday to plan a date for Friday and he doesn't end up calling until Thursday. Resist the temptation to ask why he didn't call earlier. He might not even know himself! He probably wasn't prepping for that call the same way you were. Men often have a different sense of time than we do. Keep it on the back burner in your mind, in case he starts to prove unreliable in other ways, but is it really that big a deal that he called late? He did call, after all. This is the type of situation in which sticking to the

FAQ

Q: A guy I went out with hasn't called me in a while. Can't I just call him to remind him that I'm around? Maybe he forgot!

A: Unless he's 92 and has Alzheimer's, he is perfectly aware of your existence and your availability.

Strategy rather than the rigid Rules is really going to pay off. If you're following the Rules, you'd probably say, "Screw him!" but I say give him a break.

You should be understanding more about men at this point. And sometimes, it's better to adopt their ways than fight them. Women will wonder why a guy doesn't express any guilt for not calling earlier. Why should he? Is it really that big a deal? Women often feel like if they don't call a friend or their mom on the particular day at the particular time they said they would, that they've done something terribly wrong. Wouldn't it be nice to just have an "I'll call when I feel like it" attitude? How incredibly liberating! Of course, it would be nice if a guy said only exactly what he meant, and everything he said was a blood promise. But since that's not the case (and not realistic either, I might add), why not cut him some slack? Just translate him using my principles. Don't expect that when he says, "I'll call you Tuesday," it's a binding contract. See when he calls, and ask yourself if you can live with his timing. Loosen your standards a little. See if he has a pattern of being overdue or if he's just a little off. It's all just a matter of degree.

On the other hand, when a guy doesn't call until Friday night at 8 p.m. for a Friday night date, and this is the second time he has done this to you, that's not a great sign. There's no point in scolding him, especially if you barely know him, but what you can do is say you've already made plans (don't just lie, either—actually make plans and have some fun despite him!). If he says, "Well, I thought we were going out," just say in a cheerful tone, "Oh, I hadn't heard from you, so I wasn't sure if we were on and something else came up. Can we try another day?" He's going to be bummed now that he hadn't called you earlier (now who's sitting home alone?!) and chances are, he'll know to be a little more conscientious next time. It doesn't mean you shouldn't go out with him again, but definitely take note. If you realize he can't be "trained" by a certain point, odds are he's not that interested in a relationship.

Advice from Dan Aferiat, Your On-Call Therapist

Why do you get so obsessed waiting for the phone to ring?

Waiting for "that" phone call can make you feel uncomfortable, anxious, depressed, and angry, because you want the kind of reassurance that you *think* only he can give you. The problem with waiting around for him to call is that it gives a man that enormous power that he doesn't deserve or really have. Needing reassurance is not the problem in and of itself. However, it is not *his* job to provide that kind of comfort in your life. You should seek that reassurance from a professional, from close friends, or even from yourself. Still, it's to be expected that you will feel overwhelmed and unsettled at times while dating. That's just part of the process.

WHEN HE CALLS

Regardless of when he calls, sound receptive and happy that he did. If you're home when he calls, by all means pick up. You don't need to act hard to get. Hopefully you won't be home, though, because you're remembering to *be* hard to get! You're probably out doing your 15 hours and being the hot commodity you always knew you were, right? Some of my Rules-following clients will wonder if they need to make a guy call them more than once before they return the call. Now, what are the odds of him calling again after not hearing from you, providing he's not a stalker? By not returning his call in a timely (i.e., within twenty-four hours) manner, you're telling him that his call doesn't mean that much to you. Unless he likes being overly aggressive, he's not going to find your behavior very attractive. He called, so he's already showing you an action that's a good sign of his interest. Why make life difficult for the guy?

If you're not available to talk, of course, don't feel like you're going to miss your only chance if you don't answer the phone. Instead of talking in furtive whispers because you happen to be at the latest Tom Cruise flick when he calls, let him leave a message and call him back from home. Another bad habit: saying "I'm busy now. Can you call me back between six thirty and seven?" He's not your employee. If you're *soooo* busy, why are you picking up the phone? Better not to pick up at all than to sound rude or hurried. You can call him back. And furthermore, why are you asking him to call *you* back, when you're the one who's unavailable? Women who do this type of thing often think they are being accommodating. For men it comes across as controlling, and that's a big turnoff.

FIND OUT WHAT KIND
OF MAN HE IS

Certain men will say things that sound like promises to make you feel safe, even if you've just met him. Top among them: "I'm not a game player." If a guy says he doesn't like playing games, odds are, he does play games. Remember that his actions mean more than his words. Just because he *says* he's different, doesn't mean he actually is. So how can you tell the talkers from the doers? By waiting and seeing what his actions are. If he says, "Let's have dinner next week!" that's a thought. If he actually calls you, that's an action. (Showing up is even more of one!) If a guy has a habit of saying flowery things like, "I want to spend a romantic week in the Caribbean," then one fun trick is to add "but not necessarily with you" at the end of each sentence. It's kind of like that game you play with fortune cookies where you add "in bed" to the end of every fortune.

Don't get too discouraged by this game, though. This exercise is only designed to help you to not get too ahead of yourself. (A lot of women are picturing walking down

This one guy I started dating went on and on from the start about how much I meant to him and how he'd do anything for me. Well, a couple of months into our relationship, it was my birthday. He said he wanted to take me out for drinks and dinner and that he was going to give me the best birthday ever. So what does he do? He arrives an hour late. I was sitting at the bar alone on my birthday. I guess as much as I meant to him, apparently his workout meant more. Oh well, at least the bartender was nice. —Erica

In My Clients' Words

the aisle as soon as the guy says anything about the future.) If the guy does prove himself with his actions, then you know that you can take him at face value. A lot of guys *do* mean it when they say nice things, so allow yourself to enjoy hearing them. It could just take some time to see if he means it. There's no need to be overly demanding or call him on everything he's said to you. You don't want to put him on the spot and make him feel cornered in the relationship before it's even begun. Let him have a chance to prove himself. Whether he does or he doesn't, you'll know soon enough what kind of man he is. But you do need to give it some time to see how things play out.

EASY DOES IT

The main complaint you hear from men is that they want relationships to be fun and easy and, so often, women won't allow that. We're always trying to analyze their every move in the relationship, interested in talking about our feelings and their feelings and what they feel about our feelings and the future and all sorts of other heavy things that most men just don't care to discuss. At the end of a tough day at work, what a guy wants to do more than anything is have a few laughs with a great girl, whether it's the first or tenth date, and forget about the stressful parts of his life for a while. The more you can be that escape for him, the more he's going to appreciate you. He's going to want to keep you in his life because you make it easier, not harder. A relationship shouldn't be a chore to either of you—not at this stage, anyway!

Now, I'm certainly not saying that he should walk all over you or that you should do everything his way. We should all have a bottom line of how we need to be treated. (Be careful that you're not expecting the unreasonable, such as long-stemmed roses every other day!) If a guy's into you, he's going to be calling you, taking you on dates, and treating you kindly and with respect. If he's not doing those things, you should dump him. Life's too short to put up with jerks. But first, make sure that his bad behavior isn't a result of your own bad behavior. If you're very controlling and demanding with how often he calls and how long you talk, for instance, that could be the reason behind his not wanting to call, or sounding curt on the phone when he does call. Lighten your hold on his reins and see what happens. Often, if you give him the room to let him initiate, you'll get much more out of him. The relationship will be better and he'll appreciate you more. The more you give him what he needs, the more he'll give back what you need.

Ever wonder to yourself: What the hell does he want?! Yes, there are going to be some men who, even though they've said they're looking for a relationship, are really only looking for sex. Whether they're still sowing their wild oats or they haven't matured to the point of being able to sustain a long-term relationship, guys in "sex mode" aren't likely to switch gears just because wonderful you has come along (although they might give it a try). Complicating matters is that a lot of men will go either way, depending on the woman's actions. If you sleep with a guy too soon, even if he's in "relationship mode," you could cause him to think *you're* the one in sex mode. And once you've given him that impression, it's pretty damn hard to change his mind again. If you've ever tried to turn a one-night stand into something more, you'll know what I'm talking about.

By letting him take the lead, you can see from his actions where he's going with you. If he seems to be rushing things sexually or if he never wants to take you on real dates but has a habit of sending you dirty e-mails, he's in sex mode. Whether a guy is in sex mode or re-

Only 2% of long-term relationships start with a one-night stand.

Fun Fact

I went on a lunch date with a guy recently who I thought was nice, but when I got up to go to the ladies' room, he had the nerve to pat me on the ass. On the first date! I was like "hello?!" —Jane

lationship mode is often something you *can* detect on the first date. One of the women I coach went out with a guy she had met online, and he was over-the-top from the start, making sexual references and being physically forward. She got swept up in the romance aspect, excited to meet a guy who was excited about her. But the relationship petered out before it even began. He never called her after their second date, probably deciding to seek out new prey rather than risk someone wanting more from him than sex.

While a guy in relationship mode is probably just as interested in sex as the guy in sex mode, he's going to be interested in a lot of other things about you, too. He'll take things slower. He'll take you on real dates and pay for many of them, your conversations won't revolve around sex, and he won't grope you after you've held up a stop sign. He's not going to use the "Can I just use your bathroom?" trick just to get into your apartment. (Have you ever fallen for that one?) Even if he can barely hold it, a relationship-minded guy will wait until he gets home rather than trying to pull a fast one on you. One of my clients learned the hard way that a guy was in sex mode by caving in to a British guy who told her that "back in London, all the girls do it on the first date," and that Americans make too big a deal about sex. She never heard from him again.

But, you ask, if a guy is in relationship mode, then how could having sex on the first date hurt? Tricky question. Not so tricky answer. If you put out on the first date, he's going to think *you're* the one in sex mode. His thought process goes from

Relationship-Mode Questions	Sex-Mode Questions
What's your favorite restaurant?	What's your favorite position?
When was your first time to New York?	When was your first time?
What's your dog's name?	Do you like it doggie style?
Is that Chanel No. 19 you're wearing?	Is that a thong you're wearing?
What's your fantasy job?	What are your sexual fantasies?

"Wow, I'd like to see this girl again" to "Whoa, that was easy! I guess she's more into just having fun right now than having a relationship."

The odds of him calling you, if you hook up on the first date, are slim. Sure, it happens. Boy meets girl, boy nails girl, boy goes out the next morning to buy the paper and bagels and returns only to never leave again. But is that really something you want to bet on? He's going to think that you do that with all the guys, no matter what you say to the contrary. Is that so wrong, you ask? Yes! Guys don't want to marry the slutty girl. It's a turnoff for them, as far as a relationship goes. Men usually take it slower when they are in relationship mode. So, if you are doing the nasty on Night One, he's probably in sex mode and very unlikely to change in the near future. There is really no way to tell how sincere a guy is on the first date. You cannot rely on his words. You have to wait and see the pattern of his

---

FAQ

Q: *What if I never want to see the guy again, but I could really use a roll in the hay?!*

A: First, make sure you're not tricking yourself, thinking that you can use sex as a way to get him to stick around. But if you truly want to use him just for his body for one night, by all means, enjoy yourself. Nothing wrong with a little side action on your way to meeting a long-term guy as long as it doesn't distract you from your goal. More on this in chapter eleven!

---

actions. Only by assessing him over time can you find out which mode he is in. But you can certainly take a guess as to his insincerity if sex is foremost in his actions on the first date.

AGE PLAYS A FACTOR

While I don't encourage you to try to change a guy from sex mode to relationship mode, men do grow and move beyond sex mode. It's not like there's one guy that's always going to be Tom Hanks and another guy is always going to be George Clooney (although George Clooney seems to be doing a great job of always being George Clooney!). Warren Beatty was in sex mode for decades, notorious for bedding everyone from Natalie Wood to Madonna. But one look at Annette Bening on the set of *Bugsy* in 1991 shot him straight into relationship mode. Or maybe he was just ready. In any case, they've been a couple ever since and have four children together. Perpetual bachelor types aside, when men are in their early to mid-twenties, they're much more likely to be focusing on their careers, and,

Advice from Dan Aferiat, Your On-Call Therapist

Do you always end up with the "wrong guys"?

If you notice that there is a problem or a pattern being repeated in your own dating life, it's not helpful to just blame the man. You must be contributing in some way to that problem. It's too simple to believe that you keep meeting the "wrong" guys, or that there are no "good" men to date. This way of thinking makes you the victim, and victims are helpless and unable to effect change. Acknowledging your contribution to the problem does not mean concluding that you are damaged goods and that you are not worthy of a relationship. It's a matter of recognizing the effects of your behavior in relationships. Becoming aware of the problem through therapy or coaching is enormously empowering, as the only person you can really control is yourself.

at that point in their lives, they often don't want anything more complicated than sex. But that could change, and it often does, when they hit thirty. The age range varies from man to man, of course, but the principle is that their mode changes as they mature and become more ready to settle down. They start seeing the men around them getting more fulfillment out of their relationships, and it stops being so scary to think of committing to one person.

Easy enough, right? While the sequence of events may vary slightly, it shouldn't veer too much off course. It's tough letting him steer, but just because he's in the driver's seat doesn't mean you can't navigate! You just need to learn how to guide him

When It's Right

Remember how I told you that there's a very specific courtship pattern that almost always leads to a lasting relationship? This is what it looks like:

- Three e-mails back and forth in each direction (if you meet on-line), in the last of which he'll ask for your number. You may hint about giving your number during that time. If you meet in person, he asks for your number when you part ways.
- One twenty-minute or so phone call, ending with him asking you out. (Talking for two hours is pointless if he doesn't ask you out, and overkill if he does.) Often, the phone call attempt is made fairly quickly (24–48 hours) after he has gotten your number.
- One date, which usually lasts a long time and is filled with lots of chemistry and ends with a passionate kiss, but not much more.
- One phone call within the next week. If it's the next day, that's a very good sign.
- Several more dates and heightened communication, building in momentum.
- One exclusivity conversation, brought up by him and usually around the same time you have sex for the first time.

The result? Two very happy people.

rather than push him. It'll be very empowering—you'll see! For instance, if you've been talking on the phone with him for a considerable amount of time with no end in sight, start to wind it down by saying you've got to run out in a few minutes (no need for him to know whether it's to get your laundry or to meet another date). But, instead of hanging up abruptly, mention again what a great time you had with him on your last date, or say that you really enjoyed talking with him. Leave a pregnant pause, long enough to make him realize that it's his move. Basically, you need to gently let him know that you've got to hang up soon, but give him five minutes to ask you out and some easy ways to do it. Some guys will ask you out in a roundabout way, too, by saying something like, "So, what are you doing this weekend?" leaving it ambiguous as to whether they are asking you out or not. My favorite response: "Why, what did you have in mind?" That way you put him back in the hot seat!

RED FLAGS

One little red flag shouldn't make you ditch a guy. But whenever there's an infraction, make a mental note to make sure it's not a pattern. One client of mine had a blind date with someone who made her wait thirty-five minutes in a restaurant alone while he searched for a parking spot. There were spots in a $5 lot right across the street, but he wanted a free spot on the street instead. Big red flag! Now, perhaps something like that is an aberration—perhaps he forgot to bring cash and the lot didn't take credit cards—but odds are he's a cheapskate and inconsiderate, and those are *not* nice traits.

Maybe your guy is rude to the waiter. There's no need to dump him because of it if he does it just once, but if he does it often, guess what? He's probably going to be pretty darn rude to you one day, too. While it's good to get a sense of what you can deal with and what you can't, first and foremost is finding a guy with good character. If you're considering spending the rest of your life with a man, you should have some respect for him as well as love.

READ THE SIGNS

Whatever comes up on the first date, there's probably a lot worse. For instance, if he says he broke up with his last girlfriend because he cheated on her, and he's not saying it with much regret or embarrassment, odds are he's done it before and he'll do it again. If it comes up a little later, though, and he says he cheated once on someone in high school and he felt so bad that he knows he'll never do it again, that's a different matter. If he's got a girlfriend—or worse, a wife—while he's on a date with you, *run!* Some guys will say that they may cheat now, but if they met the right girl, they'd never cheat. That's rarely the case. Chronic cheaters never meet the right girl because the right girl would never put up with a louse like that! Resist the temptation to think that your connection is so strong that it will overcome his tendency to cheat. Cheaters are hard-wired that way. It'll take a lot more help than you in his life (like some major therapy) to make him quit screwing around.

NO SETTLING

What you can put up with and what you can't is going to be a matter of personal preference. Just don't feel like you have to put up with something that's a major cause of distress just because you're worried there's no one better out there. You will be absolutely miserable if you don't feel safe and secure with the guy you're with. Do you want to look forward to your wedding day or do you want to dread it? You deserve happiness, so if you think someone is going to fall way short of that, keep looking. He's out there! You just have to find him!

O*kay, so it's not* quite as romantic as reaching for the same bunch of grapes at the market or bumping into each other on a train. But you never know how it's going to happen for you. As much as I want you to hope for a serendipitous run-in with Mr. Wonderful (if you have your Cablight on, anything is possible!), online dating can be a great practical way to help romance along. The Internet is right at your fingertips, first of all, so it can be an easy way to get started in dating, especially if you're shy. In the end, it really doesn't matter *how* you met, anyway. Only that you did! There is a technique to online dating that you need to learn in order to make it work for you, though.

I've had a lot of clients tell me they've tried Internet dating but that it didn't work for them. When I delve further into it with them, there's usually a common pattern to their Internet experience. It goes something like this: "Well, I found the only digital picture that I had of myself, so I uploaded it and filled out the profile. . . . I don't really remember what I said about myself. A ton of guys wrote almost as soon as I posted it and I ended up going out with a couple, but they were *total losers*. Then I went searching through profiles myself and found two or three cool guys. So I wrote to them but they never wrote me back! I just got discouraged by the whole thing, so I took my profile down."

Sound familiar? First of all, this is not giving online dating a fair shot. People think that it should be as simple as a click of the mouse, but there's still a process that you have to follow. You have to be patient and use it strategically. In order to get to the "quality guys" (i.e., the good catches), you need a few lessons in mastering the art of online dating. When a client tells me, "I've tried online dating and it doesn't work!" I tell them the same thing a director tells an actor after a dull scene: "Now do it again, but with *feeling!*" You have got to do this with feeling or you'll never get your own Oscar—or Tom or Keith or Brent! When the same clients try online dating my way, they get completely different results. One client of mine was a bit hesitant about trying online dating again, because she had tried it in the past unsuccessfully. Once she took my advice on how to write a profile and what type of picture she should use, she said it was like "turning on a faucet!" So forget everything you've experienced in the past. You're going to be armed with my Strategy this time.

> **Quick Tip**
>
> *I recommend being on two sites simultaneously. Choose one mainstream site and one that's smaller and more specific to your interests. And don't be a cheapskate! Most sites cost only about $20 or so a month. That's nothing! A lot of guys spend that on the tip alone for one date, so you're getting off easy. Invest in your future—it's worth it.*

YOUR PROFILE

Think: Descriptive. Enticing. Engaging. The biggest problem with most online profiles is that they're *waaaay* too bland. Instead of taking the risk of turning a few people off, women will often be very conservative with their profiles. (When you try to please everyone, you often please no one.) For example, everyone says, "I love to travel" or "I like to be active" or "I'm looking for someone to share my life with." *Boring!* The more bland you appear in your profile, the more bland the guys are who are going to respond—if any. There's a lot of competition out there, so you need to separate yourself from the pack in your online ad by posting an eye-catching picture of yourself and writing a memorable profile. Your goal in online dating is not to attract every single guy who looks at your profile. Just the right ones. Instead of playing "not to lose," as you may have in the past, you're going to play to *win* this time!

THE PHOTO

The photo is 90% of what guys look at in a profile, so it can't just be any photo—it has to be really good. I know that looks shouldn't matter and it's not fair, blah blah blah . . . but the fact is, looks do matter, especially to men. Instead of complaining about it, you might as well accept it. Remember when I asked you if you want it to be fair or if you want to be happy? Also know that just because looks matter, doesn't mean you need to look like Rebecca Romijn. You can be overweight or quirky-looking and still take a beautiful picture. You just have to have your Cablight on! So instead of going to D.C. to lobby against

I'm 37 and plus-sized, but it's all about your attitude and how you feel about yourself that makes you ready to find the One. I'd been through some less than wonderful dating experiences in the past. But I decided to turn on my Cablight and posted ads on Match.com and Yahoo personals. Shortly thereafter, I met a wonderful man. He's sweet, charming, interesting, exuberant, intelligent, family oriented, and a great kisser—in short, everything I'd ever hoped for, and more than I ever even dreamed of. Five months after dating, he proposed! —Debra

the superficiality of it all, make the smarter move by setting up a mini photo shoot with a friend and a digital camera.

THE PHOTO SHOOT

When you do your photo shoot, find a pal to play photographer who makes you feel relaxed and brings out a smile in you. If you need a little help calming your nerves, have a glass or two of wine to make the experience more fun. And don't use your friend's excuses for canceling as your excuse. If your modeling session keeps getting pushed off, ask another friend to help. Or better yet: Go to a professional. (Just make sure they make it look natural, not like the head shot of someone auditioning for *Days of Our Lives*.)

Whatever you do, don't settle for some random jpeg you have on your hard drive. Sure, it may seem contrived to take photos specifically for your online dating profile, but who cares? A guy will notice your eyes, your smile, and whether you are looking at the camera. He'll imagine you're looking at him. He's not going to be thinking about who's taking the picture and why.

Top Ten Points on Being Picture-Perfect

10. Wear something flattering, maybe with a hint of cleavage. While you don't want to look slutty, you don't want to hide your body, either.

9. Enjoy a drink or two during your shoot. It will help you loosen up.

8. Shoot outside if you can. (But no need to be a martyr if it's minus ten degrees out!) Natural light is the most flattering, so head out to the backyard or in front of a big window. Your picture will also look less posed this way.

7. Make eye contact with the lens.

6. Reveal yourself. Have your Cablight on—look a little vulnerable.

5. Try to say something with your smile by making it alluring. A smile without showing your teeth is the best look for most people.

4. Easy on the makeup. If you're Ivana-Trumped up, you may look the way your mother tells you to look, but not the way a guy would want you to look. Don't use a photo from the last glitzy suburban wedding you attended, either.

3. Pretend you're doing your *Playboy* pictorial (only clothed). Think about something sexy when you pose.

2. Take your time and do multiple close-ups and full-length shots. Narrow down the choices later on your computer.

1. When you're deciding on a photo, pick shots that have the most life to them. Look for that Cablight in yourself!

CHOOSING THE PHOTO

Post one face shot and one full-body shot. Yes, you need the body shot. It's what guys want to see, so flaunt what you have. Wear something that's a little low cut or that shows off your legs. Pick one or the other, so you don't look overly sexy. You should also be wearing different outfits in your two shots, so it doesn't look like you did it all in one day. Here's a tip I often give my clients before they have their photo taken: Pick up a Victoria's Secret catalog and look at the models' faces. See how they draw you in with their eyes and a hint of a smile? Some poses are a little too sultry, of course—and I don't recommend being photographed in a bra!—but Heidi Klum and her pals really know how to captivate an audience with their eyes, even in 2-D. Practice in front of the mirror to find an expression that makes you look more than just pretty—your goal is to make those pictures come alive!

THE TEXT

Your main goal in writing the text of your profile is to give guys plenty of openings to respond to. The more descriptive your profile, the easier it's going to be for a guy to write to you. It's like giving him an icebreaker. Ideally, you want to be playful, lively, fun, and intriguing. For instance, instead of saying you love "travel" and "great conversation" (is there anyone online who doesn't say they love those things?), make what you write more memorable and easy to respond to by saying that you'd much rather go backpacking in the Chilean Patagonia than go to Club Med, or why you can't wait to go to Rio this spring.

Instead of saying you love music, name some bands that you listen to or recent concerts that you've been to. At Drip, my dating café, I can't tell you how many profiles I came across where people listed their musical preference as "anything but country." How boring is that? Choice in music can say a lot about a person, so dig a little deeper and say what you love. Don't think about whether the guy reading it is going to have the same affection for 50 Cent or U2 as you do. It doesn't matter (unless we're talking Celine Dion). The point is to add some life to

---

Exercise

Use this space to write down the things that make you *you*, without imagining whether guys will think you're weird or have bad taste. Maybe you have a black belt in martial arts. Or you have a collection of *Jetsons* memorabilia. Maybe you did a stint in the Peace Corps or you were the junior archery champion of Ohio when you were a kid. Jot anything down you can think of that can paint a good, colorful picture of you.

_____

_____

_____

_____

_____

_____

Boring	Interesting
I love animals.	I have two Great Danes named Starsky and Hutch.
Traveling is fun.	My best vacation was bicycling through the south of France.
I like going out on weekends.	Me + two drinks + microphone = bad karaoke.
I like to listen to music.	I can't be in a bad mood if Blink-182 is on my iPod.
I'm pretty liberal.	Michael Moore in '08!
I'm close with my family.	With five older brothers, I was born to be a football fan.
I'm competitive.	I'll bet you $20 I can kick your ass at Boggle.

your profile and give him something to comment on or ask you about.

Even your handle or member name can give guys an opening. One client of mine called herself Tuesday Girl (she decided on that because she wanted a guy she could kick back with on a boring ol' Tuesday night, not just Fridays and Saturdays) and it ended up being a great opening for a lot of the guys who wrote to her. It offers a teaser of information to pique their curiosity.

Now, of course there are going to be guys out there who look at your profile, see "Peace Corps," and immediately move on because they don't want "that type" of girl. But that's a good thing. While you may see this as scaring guys off, what you're really doing is weeding out the wrong guys. You're not looking for just anyone. You're looking for a guy who's going to be the right fit for you. If a guy is going to score points against you for being in the Peace Corps or liking foreign films, then odds are he's not a guy you're really going to get along with anyway. Besides, if a guy likes most of what you have to say, then no one thing is going to blow it. So have fun with writing all about you on your profile and imagine that great guy stumbling across it and thinking you're perfectly awesome.

SHOW YOUR ASSETS

Some women are concerned about coming across as too vain or cocky, so they undersell instead, saying they have an "okay" job when they're a VP. Or saying they like horseback riding when they actually compete in equestrian shows. On the flip side, you can run the risk of sounding vain if you say things like "I have such a *fabulous* life and *amazing* friends and a *fantastic* career!" Too perfect can be scary for a guy. I saw a show once where they interviewed a lot of the former Miss Americas, and most of them are single! There's such a thing as being too poised. It's important to show a balance of imperfections and vulnerability along with all the good stuff. Don't downgrade yourself (it's good to be confident), but don't go overboard and brag, either. Find the middle ground.

Also, avoid going

> **Quick Tip**
>
> *Do a spell check before you post your profile. It shows poor Netiquette when you ask someone to read something with bad grammar, no punctuation, or bad spelling. And ALL CAPS sounds like you're YELLING. A sloppy profile shows that you don't care.*

on and on and on about yourself. You don't need to tell your life story in your profile, or share every single like and dislike. A few sentences for each section is plenty. More than that and you'll come off as narcissistic. Leave him wanting to know more about you, not less. Plus, if you seem like the type who won't shut up about herself, he'll dread going on a date with you.

ELIMINATE THE NEGATIVE

Now, while I want you to be detailed about the unique and cool stuff about you and your life, you don't need to mention the negative stuff. He doesn't need to know, for instance, that you used to be overweight or you're in AA, or that you're in between jobs. This is, after all, an advertisement, not an obligation on your part for full disclosure of all your faults and foibles. Everyone has negative traits that may or may not come out throughout the course of a relationship, but why sabotage your chances at even a first date? Keep your reader in mind as you're writing your profile. Try to read between your own lines and make sure that you're giving a positive picture of yourself. It's best not even to joke about negative stuff, unless you're confident that you can pull it off. To anyone who doesn't know your sense of humor, you're going to come off as more unstable than funny. Humor, especially self-deprecating humor, is sometimes hard to read on the page—this goes for e-mailing, too—so you run the risk of your reader not knowing it's a joke. If you do want to make a crack about something in your profile, add a little smiley ☺ or a "(just kidding!)" beside it to make sure it's clear you're joking around. Note: Men who are self-deprecating, on the other hand, tend to be better catches than the ones who brag.

There is a difference between being negative and showing

When You Say You're . . .	He's Going to Think You're . . .
"Rubenesque," "voluptuous," or "curvy"	Fat
"Refined"	A snob
"Into fine dining"	Looking for a meal ticket
"Ready to settle down"	In a rush to get married
"Looking for a guy who respects my feelings"	Bitter from a past relationship

vulnerability. For example, showing vulnerability is saying "I loved snorkeling in Tahiti but I haven't been brave enough to go scuba diving yet." Being negative is saying "I don't go to the beach much because I'm afraid of the water." Reread your profile to make sure you haven't inadvertently put in negative things, either. You know how when you're looking for a new house or apartment, there are clues in the real estate ad about the condition it's in? "Cozy" means it's absurdly small, for instance, and "lots of charm" usually means it's in need of "lots of renovation." Same thing with online profiles. Some of the words you use could give the wrong impression.

THE VULTURES

Once you've posted your profile, you may find yourself swamped with e-mails very early on. Be flattered, but weed through these

One of the things I've learned is that I need to give myself permission to be mean. I'm a good girl and I always thought I had to reply to every person who contacted me online. But I don't feel like I have to now. My time is too valuable. It's tough at first, because you feel like you're being rude, but the more you do it, the more you get used to it. —Susan

carefully. These guys are what I call the "vultures." In all likelihood, they've been on the site you're using for years, glued to their computers every night just waiting for "fresh blood." These guys are often pretty crippled when it comes to actual dating, though. Often, they're looking for a pen pal, or they just want to see if they can "hook you in," but rarely will they make it to actually calling you or going on an actual date. Their notes to you will often be pretty simple, like, "Hey, what's up?" or something along those lines. They'll often use Instant Messenger rather than e-mailing. I advise you not to answer any IM messages, unless you really can't resist the guy. The risk with IM is that you'll get hooked into wasting a lot of time before knowing if a guy is worth it. It also breeds a familiarity that you should avoid before going on a first date with someone. If a guy contacts you through IM, just close the window and forget about it.

DO THE PICKING

Hopefully, you'll get non-vultures writing you, too, but you can't rely on that. It's flattering to be chosen, but I find that the guys you pick are usually the better ones. So don't just sit there! For whatever reason, the good guys don't have to have their Cablights on for very long. So you need to act fast when you see someone you like. I know you like to be pursued, but it doesn't work to wait to be pursued online. Otherwise all the pushy J.Lo types will snatch up all the great catches! You don't have to be aggressive or actually ask the guys out. All I'm asking is for you to carve out a few sentences to make him aware of your existence. In the end, he probably won't even remember who picked whom first. You just make the initial contact and then let him lead from there. Please don't only rely on the site to do the searching for you, either. Just because Match.com might say you're compatible with WildOatsBill, for instance, doesn't mean he's for you. It's more likely that the site decided to link you up just because you're in the same zip code.

I had tried J Date for years, but the only attention I got was from these boring, nebbishy guys that I never even wanted to go out with. As soon as I started to pick the guys, I had much more activity and a much better "caliber" of dates. —Ellen

In My Clients' Words

PICK TEN

Now you're going to pick ten guys and e-mail them. Yes, ten. Ten per week. It's important to cast a wide net. (Collect all the fish first, then throw the ones you don't want back in!) If you don't want to go out with a guy again after you've met, that's one thing, but there's a difference between being discriminating after you've met someone and being *picky* before you've met. Go out with as many guys as you can, especially at first. Even give all the "maybes" a shot. If anything intrigues you in a guy's profile, write to him. And don't make the mistake of having different standards online than you do in "real life" when filling in your criteria. Sometimes, if a girl is dating online, she might *only* search for guys six feet tall and over, for instance, but if she's at a bar and a cute, short guy approaches, she's open to it. Or she might restrict her online search to guys who make $100,000 a year, but when offline, she frequently falls for the starving-artist type. I call this the Proactive vs. Reactive phenomenon. When women are being proactive in dating (i.e., doing the choosing), they're far more picky than if they're in the reactive position of guys approaching them. Think of what flaws you can live with and what you really can't. For instance, would you really care if a guy was sweet, successful, and smart, but maybe he didn't have *all* his hair? If you're too picky about certain traits, you're going to miss out on some other more important ones. Stick to your instincts on traits that are deal-breakers for you, though. Maybe it's crucial that you meet someone who's Catholic, for instance, or someone who loves the beach. It is okay to be picky with some things, just not everything.

> **In My Clients' Words**
>
> *I think I finally found a great guy because I learned what is important in a life partner. It's way more than just gorgeous packaging. It's goodness and humor and kindness and caring and patience and generosity of spirit. —Laura*

JUST SAY YES

Don't look for reasons to rule someone out before you've even met him. You often can't figure out if someone's for you unless you meet the guy. It's really all about chemistry. Also, try to tolerate as much as you can as far as age and height. For instance, maybe you think anyone over 40 is too old for you. Have you never met someone who's 40 and looks like he's 30? It might not matter to you as much as you think if you meet a guy who has a young spirit. I'm only asking that you not make assumptions based on arbitrary traits. Once you meet the men in question, you *can* form opinions. If what you believe about 40-year-olds or cat owners or accountants holds true when you meet them, then it's okay not to go out with the guy again. But as a general rule, just cast a wide net and say yes to every potential date. That way you won't miss out on someone who could be really good, just because he didn't fit your "search criteria." One of my clients in her late forties aims for guys between 45 and 58, but if someone younger contacts her (she's had responses from guys as young as 28!), she'll go out with them anyway. "What the hell?" she says. "If I don't like them for a relationship, I'll just go for the sex!"

G.U. (GEOGRAPHICALLY UNDESIRABLE)

Although I want you to widen your criteria whenever possible, I don't recommend you go far outside your geographic area. Some people go so far as to fly to another city to meet someone. If someone writes to you from another city, nip it in the bud. Say something like, "I'd love to meet you the next time you're in Chicago," or wherever you live. If

> *The thing that's great about online dating is that it sends you so much hope. You never know who's out there or who's going to wink at you. And there's always this sense of excitement when you check your e-mail. Even if I'm not that interested in anyone, just logging in always gives me a great boost.*
> —Lisa

In My Clients' Words

he's willing to come to you and has a place to stay, then great. Otherwise, you're probably wasting your time. Long-distance relationships are hard enough for people who have been to-gether for years. They're close to impossible for couples who haven't even met.

THE I IN 10 RULE

When you're sending your e-mails, don't overthink them or feel the need to choose one guy over another. If he seems to have any potential at all, just e-mail him! Chances are, only one of these ten e-mails is going to lead to a date, anyway, and you never know which one it will be. That's why it's important to cast such a wide net. Don't put off e-mailing guys, either, by putting them on a "favorites" list or a "hot list," as some sites have. That's my biggest pet peeve about online dating. Just go for it—don't waste time procrastinating. Even if you do end up having a date with a guy you're not that wild about, it's only forty-five minutes of your life. You can—and should—take that risk. Another thing to keep in mind is that sometimes a guy can be very different from his profile (hence the *huge* importance of meeting in person). That dreamy guy in the Yankees T-shirt? It's just as likely that he's as wrong for you as the nerdy, shy-looking guy is right for you. So give *any* guys a shot that you might consider, and see what happens.

Go for some guys who might be hotter than you, too. Why not, right? Just don't get upset at rejection at this level. It's only e-mail! The guy hasn't even met you, so he's not rejecting the real you—just the paper version. Besides, you never know why someone isn't writing you back. He could have a girlfriend now, or maybe he's in sex mode and he sees that you're a relationship kind of girl. He could even just be online for an ego boost.

While I want you not to be intimidated by the very handsome ones, don't limit yourself to them. Try also for the friendly-looking guys who have a spark in their eyes. Someone's picture does say a lot. (Now that you're checking out the guys' pictures, you see why your own is so important!) You'll just get a feeling of whether you could see yourself going out with a guy or not. Trust your gut on this one. If he looks warm, happy, unpreten-

Tips on Reading His Profile	
Good	**Not So Good**
Short and sweet answers.	Rambling and/or bragging.
Self-deprecating humor.	Crude humor.
Mentions his love of movies.	Mentions his love of big boobs.
Solo photo of him.	Photo of him with his date cut out of the picture.
He's smiling and has warm eyes.	He's in an Arnold Schwarzenegger pose with sunglasses on.
He says he's looking for a relationship.	He says he's looking "just for fun" (code for sex mode).
He's either single or divorced.	He's separated (he could still be living with his wife).

tious, and like someone you think you'd at least like to talk to if you met him out at a party, then go for it.

E-MAILING

So what do you say? You don't want the e-mail you send to sound canned. At the same time, you don't want to spend all day writing a lengthy missive to him, either. (This shouldn't take up your entire 15 hours a week!)

The formula for success? Three sentences, as follows:

1. Comment on one thing about his profile that you can relate to. It will make him feel special and it shows you have something in common. Guys like to feel singled out just as much as we do.
2. Write a sentence about yourself that shows your personality and gives him a clue as to why you are responding to his profile.
3. End with a question. It's hard for someone to resist a question, so asking one will help draw him in and get him to respond to you.

Here's an example: "I see you like downhill skiing. Every year I tell myself I should at least *try* snowboarding, but I'm devoted to my skis. Have you ever gone to the dark side?"

If you want to comment on a joke he made in his profile as well, or perhaps an interesting observation he made, that's great, too. Be a little flirty and playful. If he says he loves vanilla ice cream, write back, "I'm a chocolate girl, myself."

Then just sign your name. Don't say anything like, "I hope to hear from you" or "Check out my profile and let me know what you think." These steps are obvious and make you sound

---

FAQ

Q: *Wouldn't it be cuter if I just sent a "wink" to a guy?*

A: No. Some online sites give the option of sending an instant message or a smiley face to someone. It's always best to send the strongest message possible, just like in the tennis game analogy—hit the ball hard. If you're too worked up about the idea of just sending an e-mail to someone, you're too afraid of rejection. Get over it!

---

weak. He knows how to find your profile—and of course he's going to check it out. Be colloquial, which will make you sound confident. Talk to him the way you would if you met him at a bar. Don't use what I call "online dating speak," which contains phrases like, "It looks like we have a lot in common!" and "I think we might be a great match!" Nope. You just sign your first name like the cool chick you are. You've hit the ball hard into his court and now it's up to him to hit it back.

One note: Although you don't want to obsess about each e-mail, you do want to read over your note before sending it. Try to put on your "man-cap" (like a thinking cap from the guy's perspective) and imagine you're the guy reading it. Keeping in mind that he's never met you, how does it come across? Sometimes you might have a hidden tone, either angry, needy, or negative, that you don't even realize is coming across. For example, "Hi, Jack. I see you're a Pistons fan. Hope that doesn't mean you don't ever have Saturday nights free! Not that I'm hinting!" (Negative, and implies you might be controlling and needy.) Something better might be: "Hi, Jack. I see you're a Pistons fan. I'm from L.A., so I'm a Lakers fan, myself. :-) Gone to any great games this season?" (Positive; gives him something about you to go on and ends with a question.) Do a quick scan to make sure you're sending the right message, then fire it off!

After shooting off your ten e-mails, just forget about it and check back in a day or two. It might take a guy a few days to a week to respond, so don't write him off or think he's rude. He could just go online occasionally, or maybe he's started going out with someone and likes to date just one woman at a time, which is admirable. (Besides, the guys that are on the site too often probably have too much time on their hands.) Don't get bogged down in how long a guy takes to respond. It's not per-

---

FAQ

Q: A guy wrote to me asking if I have any more pictures of myself. Isn't that rude?

A: Not really. In all likelihood, he's trying to get a better sense of your body type, especially if you don't already have a full-length shot up. This is direct, but not necessarily rude. A lot of guys are looking for a very distinct physical type. E-mail him a photo that shows your figure a little better. Even if you are overweight, don't sweat it. Send the picture and forget about it. For every guy who doesn't like voluptuous women, there's another one who does. Don't take it personally. He's actually doing you a favor by not wasting your time. If he showed up for the date and then was rude based on your looks, that would be worse. And it's okay to ask yourself if you're up for being scrutinized like that. If he's being that picky, then he may be too focused on looks, which may not be right for you. But don't blame him. Just use the information as data about him that you can evaluate.

sonal. He doesn't even know you, so it's not about you. Also, don't romanticize and get hung up on *one* guy that you wrote to. Chances are, he's not the guy you think he is, anyway. Let yourself be surprised by everyone. You'll have more fun this way and you'll be less disappointed. When the guys do respond, you should weed out any who write back anything explicitly sexual. These guys are in sex mode. It's easy to make the mistake of thinking that some of these comments are sexy; they may even turn you on. But I have found that the type of guy who is that open about sex online is often weird in person. He should have enough of a sense of boundaries to have some semblance of privacy about sex. Even if you happen to rate sex pretty highly and are a sexually adventurous person yourself, that type of information should come out a few dates down the road with someone, not before you've even met him. Any guy who gets too steamy at the e-mail stage, whether it's saying, "Hey, sexy" or "What's your body like?" doesn't have very high standards. He's likely saying this to every girl online, just to see what he can get. Furthermore, he's probably not the faithful type. Hold out for a good guy with other interests who happens to be great in bed, not a guy who only wants to talk about sex.

GET TO THE DATE

So what happens when a guy writes back something sweet or funny or cute? That's great! Respond with another note about the same length as his, answering any questions he has and maybe asking another couple of light ones of your own in return. Keep things flirty, fun, and playful. It's like banter at a bar when you've first met someone, only it's with e-mail.

As I mentioned earlier, the normal protocol is about three e-mails in each direction until he asks for your phone number, and one phone conversation (about twenty minutes, optimally) that's light and breezy and ends in him asking you out. The whole thing from first contact to first date is usually around two weeks. Don't trust the guys who rush into wanting to meet in person before a level of rapport is reached. A lot of people think they'll just meet the very next day for drinks, but there's a courtship process online that needs to take place. The e-mails back and forth help create a comfort level, as does the phone call. If you do get to the phone stage with someone, odds are about 90% that you'll go on a date with him (unless the conversation is so bad you don't want to anymore!). It's inevitable that you're going to run into guys who just want to e-mail indefi-

---

Advice from Dan Aferiat,
Your On-Call Therapist

Why is it so easy to "click" with someone online, only to be disappointed in person?

It's easy to fall in love online because you have no real data (other than what is in your own mind) with which to formulate who this man is. The conscious part of your mind might envision your potential partner as rich, funny, tall, handsome, kind, etc. . . . all the perfect ideals you are searching for. Unconsciously, you may be wondering if you will be his ideal. The longer you go without actually meeting, the more you maintain the illusion that you would be great partners together and end up in love. You need the real-life data of meeting the person to offset those illusions. If you have never met, you have no facts to go on. It is all simply fantasy. Fantasy is impossible to live up to, for both partners.

nitely, never getting around to asking for your phone number or for a date. If things don't appear to be escalating toward an encounter off the computer, he's likely wasting your time. If you've exchanged three e-mails each way, and he hasn't asked for your number, here are some ways to try to move it from e-mail to the phone.

1. Hint by saying, "Don't you find e-mailing when we've never met to be kind of strange?"
2. Start being slow to respond to his e-mails (take a few days).
3. In your next reply, type in your phone number after you sign your name.
4. Be direct. Say, "If you want to call me, here's my number." If he doesn't call you or ask you out at that point, it's time to move on. Don't bother answering any more of his e-mails. He's clearly more into virtual relationships than real ones.

PHONE TAG

It's good to aim for a phone conversation before you have a date with someone. Some guys will try to set up something over e-mail, which is okay, but at least get each other's phone numbers in case someone is running late or needs to reschedule. It's harder for him to stand you up if he's got your number! Odds are, he will ask for your phone number in the course of your e-mails to give you a call first, though. Then the phone tag begins. Don't worry if it takes a few phone calls to connect, and don't fall into the habit of giving a specific time for him to call. This comes across as controlling, and it sets you up to be waiting by the phone. Then, if he doesn't call when you told him to, you already feel rejected. But maybe he just wasn't free at that time. You may defend yourself by thinking you were being accommodating by telling him when you would be home, but so what if you're not home when he calls? It's not like he can't or won't call you again.

Phone tag is an important part of the process. It can even be exciting playing the back-and-forth voice mail game. Don't pick up the phone unless you can talk. It's not good to sound rude. You want to seem excited to hear from him. Try to make yourself available before the phone tag goes too long, though. Phone tag can only go so many rounds (about three times back and forth) before it loses momentum. When you finally do reach each other, try to spend about twenty minutes or so talking. It can be very tempting to chat all night if you have great phone banter, but the purpose of the phone call is to set up a date. It shouldn't be a date in and of itself.

When it's time to wrap things up, it's okay to be the one to end the call, but don't be abrupt. Say something like, "Well, it was good to be able to hear your voice . . ." or "It was really nice talking with you . . ." but be sure to say it in a way that leaves a pregnant pause at the end. (It's "pregnant" because the moment is pregnant with the possibility of him asking you out!) You can even do something simple during a lull in the conversation by apologetically saying, "I kinda have to go, but I've really had fun talking to you. . . ." and see what he does. It gives him his cue, like a script in a play. If he's struggling with asking you out, be flirty with him and give him openings. For example, talk about the places you like to go, or things you like to do that you might want to do with him. It's not always a piece of cake for a guy, so any way you can make it easier for him will help. If he doesn't ask you out, don't panic. It's possible he'll do it via e-mail or he'll call back tomorrow—he might be a little gun-shy. Or, he might be chickening out. If so, good riddance. It's better not to ask him out, because you'll find out more about him that way. But it isn't out of the question. If you find that he's extremely shy (and you don't mind shy guys) or if you think *you* may have come across

Don't waste a weekend night on an Internet date. It's great to hope for the best, but odds are against you that there will be chemistry, and you might resent blowing your Saturday night on someone you didn't click with. Besides, weekend nights are prime time for meeting other guys!

Quick Tip

as aloof, then you could do the asking. If you happen to hang up without a date scheduled, don't give up, but don't hold your breath. Odds are, he will ask you out on the phone call, though. Like I said, if your e-mails have led to a phone call, there's a 90% chance that the phone call will lead to a date. As for scheduling, if he has a day in mind and you're free, say yes. No need to play games, pretending you're busy when you're not. If he puts the ball in your court, give him three times that will work for you. That way, one of them should work for him, and you won't seem too busy or restrictive with your schedule. An after-work drink is often best for a blind date, which I'll explain more about in the next chapter, but the point is to give him a few scheduling options and then let him choose. He might have something more fun in mind, to which I say, "Why not?"

FANTASY VS. REALITY

One problem you might run into online are guys who fall in love with you right away, before you've even met. This is a sure sign of a loser. He's falling in love with his fantasy of you, not

---

Internet Dating Safety Tips

- Give him a number where you can be reached, but don't give your last name.
- Arrange to meet at a public place in a neighborhood that you know.
- Meet him there rather than have him pick you up.
- Limit yourself to one or two drinks so you don't lose your senses.
- Never go to his place on the initial meeting, no matter how nice he seems.
- Hope for the best, but plan for the worst.

---

the real you. That's why it's so important to meet the guys from online after a few breezy e-mails and a light phone conversation. If it gets any heavier than that, you may fall into the same trap of confusing fantasy and reality. One client of mine, before I started working with her, got so swept up in a phone conversation with a guy she'd met online—talking for far longer than the twenty minutes I recommend—that they ended up having phone sex! When they met in person for lunch the next day, she found she wasn't even remotely attracted to him. Needless to say, it was a very awkward meal. This is an extreme case, but the point is to not share too much of yourself, either emotionally or sexually, before you meet someone. Keep it light.

It can be very tempting to think that because you have an incredible e-mail or phone rapport with someone, you're "meant to be." Don't make this mistake. It's not a good idea to go on any date thinking he's going to be the man of your dreams. You can hope, but don't decide beforehand. As I've said, keep your hopes high, but your expectations low. It's a blind date like any other, no matter how dreamy he seems over e-mail or on the phone. It's a big temptation to want to go from not knowing someone to *Boom!* being in a relationship, but this is a step-by-step process. So, if any kind of discussion of this sort comes up before you meet, like, "Oh, we're so perfect for each other!" or "You're all I've ever dreamed of!" change the subject or you both could be woefully disappointed. Keep an air of polite distance between you in the e-mail and pre-date phone call stages. Deep thoughts or emotions shouldn't be discussed; same with the topics of sex, past relationships, any traumas you've had in your life, or your hopes for marriage and children. This stuff is all too much too soon. Remember: You have never met. But hopefully . . . you're about to!

9

The Big Date

Okay, so you've finally gotten to the exciting part! The big date. Now, I want you to go into it hopeful, but don't take it personally if you don't click. In fact, your odds of clicking, especially if your first date is also the first time you're meeting, are only about 1 in 10. You can improve those odds, though. If you employ the right strategy, you'll improve your hit rate for a second date. You know that expression, "You never get a second chance to make a first impression"? It's especially true in dating. So your goal on a first date with someone should be to knock his socks off. Even if you're not sure you like him, you always want to have the option. After all, wouldn't you rather be the one making the decision?

SETTING UP THE DATE

A lot of people try to put too much pressure on a first date by making a big production of it. For a blind date, a simple after-work drink often works best. It's easy, it's casual, and it doesn't have to take all night. In case you don't like him and want to keep things short, you can also convincingly tell him you have plans afterward. So if he asks what you'd like to do, an after-work drink could be your suggestion. Drinks or coffee will take the pressure off of him, too, since he'll be relieved to know he doesn't have to plan and pay for dinner with a woman he's never met. If he likes you, he'll probably ask you to dinner during the date. But let's hope for now that he's the one doing the suggesting, so all you need to do is let him lead (remember the tennis game?). Often, he will suggest a drink for the same reasons described above. Most important, be flexible when he's asking you out. That counts for what you're doing as well as when you do it. If he asks when you're available, give him two to three choices. You don't want to come across as controlling by only giving him one night as an option. At the same time, you don't want to seem like you have nothing on your schedule besides *Sex and the City* reruns, either, by saying "I'm available whenever you want!"

HOPES HIGH, EXPECTATIONS LOW

Whatever you end up doing, don't go into the date assuming he's going to be the love of your life. Hedge your bets, but at the same time, don't go into the date with a pessimistic attitude. Keep your hopes high, but your expectations low, remember? Don't plan for the worst by wearing a boring outfit, either. One of my clients had two dates lined up, one with a guy she thought showed huge promise and another that she thought would be a dud. So she wore her best date outfit for the first, whom she ended up not being attracted to, and a not-so-hot outfit to the second, who ended up being way more of a catch than she imagined. She started looking her best on every date after that. Along the same lines, hope that you will go out to dinner right afterward if things are going well by not making plans to do something an hour later. I would recommend eating something before the date, though, so that you're not feeling starved if you don't go out to dinner. You don't want to sit there pounding back drinks on an empty stomach. If you're prepared for anything, it's a lot easier to be spontaneous and to let him lead.

Quick Quiz

So he chooses where to go . . . and it's Starbucks.

Do you:

a) run in the other direction
b) insist on better
c) go with the flow

Okay, so it's not very sexy. And there is a possibility that he may be very cheap or not at all creative, but give him the benefit of the doubt. Perhaps he's not a big drinker. Maybe he's not sure if you are. Or maybe he's been on so many dates lately that his wallet—and ego—are running on empty. Just meet him for the damn coffee (c—go with the flow). If he's not the man you thought he was, you're outta there before you can say "grande half-caf mocha latte." And if he is, there's probably a more romantic setting just around the corner where you may end up afterward!

Quick Quiz

So he chooses where to go . . . and it's the most romantic restaurant in the city followed by a carriage ride and then front row seats at a jazz club.

Do you:

a) run in the other direction (you'd actually prefer Starbucks!)
b) insist on less
c) go with the flow

Okay, so you're a little wary of spending five hours plus with a virtual stranger, but what the heck! If you really can't stand him, you can always scoot home before the carriage ride, saying your allergies are acting up or something. It is always good to go with the flow. Even if you don't think he's the guy for you, it's free dinner! If he's not such a perfect guy, remember, it can still be a lot of fun to go on a perfect date. The point is that you don't know whether or not he's a great guy until you have the date, anyway. The case where I'd say you should insist on less is if you don't feel safe enough with him to commit to the enchanted evening he has in mind. (Midnight walk through a cornfield with a stranger? Not so safe!) In those cases, it's fine to say something like, "Let's start with a drink and take it from there," so that you leave yourself an out. Don't make a big production out of why you're downsizing the date. Just say you're already going out late a couple of nights this week but you really do want to meet him sooner rather than later. As a side note, however, it *is* a bit of an odd sign if he plans a five-hour date before you've even met. It implies that he doesn't have that many dates. Or that he's a crash-and-burn type, who does all he can to impress you and then suddenly disappears. But *planning* a five-hour first date is different than *having* a five-hour first date. When a date starts off as drinks and he suggests more places to go because he is enjoying your company, that is a very good sign.

WHAT TO WEAR . . .

The key is to look cute, not cold. So ditch the suit! This isn't a job interview. And show off "the goods," whatever they may be. You don't have to reinvent the wheel on what works with men! Forget how much you spent on your new Jil Sander button-down. If you look hotter in that clingy J. Crew top you bought at the factory outlet, wear that. Sex sells, so while you're

Quick Tip

Don't wear pantyhose with open-toed shoes. You don't want to remind him of his great-aunt Lois.

not going to *have* it on the first date, you do want to *allude* to it, subtly, of course. If you've got a great chest, whip out that V-neck cashmere sweater. Even a tight-fitting turtleneck can be sexy. But most guys, besides Carson Kressley, really couldn't care less who designed it. An Old Navy halter top beats a Gucci caftan any day. Do what works for you. If great legs are your best feature, do heels and a little skirt. Hooker boots and a sequined bra aren't the best idea, but short of that, don't start worrying, "What kind of girl will he think I am?" As long as you don't behave overly sexy, you're okay with looking sexy. Let him see that you're a sexual person while at the same time making it clear that you're not ready to act on it—*yet*.

Jessica Simpson is a good example of someone who learned how to take advantage of her physical attributes, without being slutty. When she was launching her career, her manager-dad was marketing her as a Christian singer and covered up her obvious sex appeal by putting her in big boxy blazers and baggy jeans. But her assets weren't limited to her incredible voice. Jessica (and her family) soon realized that you can look sexy without being all about sex. When she

In My Clients' Words

To get my energy and confidence up for a first date, I always listen to my iPod on the way to meeting the guy. A couple of my favorites that always make me feel sexier are Pink and Pat Benatar. It works every time. —Sandy

---

FAQ

Q: My friend told me I should always show up ten minutes late for a date to make him sweat it a little.

A: No. That's just rude. You wouldn't appreciate a guy being late. You'd think he was a jerk. Being on time will show him you're the reliable, polite girl he wants to meet. Men will tolerate lateness at first, if they are interested, but they get tired of it pretty quickly. It shows that you don't value his time. If you get there early, order yourself a drink and start chatting with the bartender. It will make him a little jealous (and regretful if he was late) and show that you're a cool, independent chick.

---

started dressing more provocatively and quit being afraid to use everything G-d gave her, look what happened! (And this is a girl who saved it until her wedding night.) Use your femininity to your advantage.

TALKING POINTS

After initial introductions, which naturally will be a little awkward—just be friendly and keep in mind that he's as nervous as you are—the conversation should go back and forth. Biggest complaint you hear from men after a first date: *She wouldn't stop talking!* Your active role should be to ask him open-ended questions about his life and what he likes to do. Get into his world and make him feel comfortable talking about it. It's good to ask about his work, in addition to his personal interests, of course, but make sure your questions are about understanding

Top Five Topics to Avoid on a First Date

5. Your meddling mother
4. Your shoplifting arrest
3. Sex
2. Past relationships
1. Marriage and kids

what he does there, not what he earns there. You know how women hate being treated like sex objects? Well, men don't want to be treated like *success* objects. If he thinks you're trying to size up his wallet, it will be a big turnoff to him.

You basically want to be light, breezy, and flirty, not like some nosy human resources interviewer who wants to know his every secret. By the same token, you shouldn't discuss any heavy topics in your own life. That means no complaining about your job, no airing of dirty family secrets or anything else that's not pleasant. Even though we all have our baggage, there's no reason to burden him with it all on a first date. Plus, you need to see if you can have fun together.

If you have any typical "guy" hobbies, this is a great topic of conversation. Maybe you're a baseball fan, you kick ass at poker, you're a pool shark, or you love golf. It's always a plus for a guy to know you have common interests. If he sees that you can enjoy some guy activities, it will be more likely that he can relate to you. And it will give him some good ideas for future dates. Vacations are also great to talk about. Everyone's been on them, they usually provide some good stories, and you both can get an idea of what the other person enjoys. After all, relationships should be all about enjoying leisure time together. Are you the camping-in-Costa-Rica type or the five-star-hotel-in-Hawaii type?

FLIRT, FLIRT, FLIRT!

As far as body language goes, show your flirty side. Run your fingers through your hair, cock your head to the side, play with your necklace. Just keep your hands off him. Some women think it's good to touch a guy's arm or knee if you like him. It's better if you don't. You could make him uncomfortable, for one. (Do you like your arm being grabbed and poked?) Let him make the first physical contact. Men enjoy the hunt, so let them! Have him aching to touch you, not praying that you would quit touching him. If you've learned how to flirt well, he's going to find you far more enticing than if you're too forward either physically or verbally. Also avoid saying anything too obvious, like, "I think we're getting along really well, don't you?" It can make for an uncomfortable moment. On reality dating shows,

---

Fun Date Idea: Playing Pool

1. It eases the tension because you're more worried about getting that #7 ball in the side pocket than saying the wrong thing.
2. Leaning over the table gives him ample opportunity to check you out.
3. You can show him that you have guy hobbies. (Quick Tip: Learn to play pool first.)
4. You can see if he's a good sport, and show that you're one, too, no matter who wins. (You may want to give him some glory in letting him kick your ass at least once, though.)

you often see women putting the man in an awkward position by saying things like, "Well, I think we have a lot in common and that we'd really be great together, don't you agree?" Those girls often don't get as far as the ones who just let the date progress naturally.

NO EX TALK!

Do not, under any circumstances, discuss your past relationships on the first date, and try your best to steer him away from talking about his. Something is wrong with him if he discusses his ex more than just mentioning her in passing. Either he's not over her or he's an oversharer! Sure, you'll naturally glean information if he brings up his own dating history without prompting, but hearing too

> *One guy I went out with kept saying, "I'm over my divorce, I really am." I was like, "Obviously you're not over it if you keep talking about it!" —Gwen*

In My Clients' Words

much about *them* before you know much else about *him* could make things confusing for you. In any case, try your hardest not to discuss your own dating history. Avoid questions on the subject in a playful way so it doesn't look like you might have some massive skeletons in your closet. Try: "Oh, this is a first date. I won't bore you with that stuff until at least the third!"

TMI

Avoid giving Too Much Information. There's this "must tell the whole truth and nothing but the truth" motto that seems ingrained in some women. *Resist!* There's no need to tell him that you haven't had sex in two years or that your last boyfriend turned out to be gay. He doesn't need to know that stuff on a first date. There's also no need to give long, involved answers when you're asked questions like, "So why are you still single?" That question drives me nuts! I tell my clients that the best way to turn it around is to give the party line answer, "I just haven't met the right guy yet." And don't look down or flinch when you say it. Men can smell vulnerability in your answer. Oftentimes, that's why they ask. In fact, you can even use the answer as a flirting tool by giving him a smirk when you say it, as a way of suggesting, "Think you're up for the challenge?" (without saying it, of course). Any first dates you've had recently aren't good conversation, either, even if they're great stories. This is a potential boyfriend, not your best girlfriend. Telling him about the guy who stuck his tongue in your ear at dinner the other night may be fun when you're both a little tipsy and you're trying to make him laugh, but the next day, it might not be so funny to him.

Quick Quiz

You're on a first date and the check comes. Do you:

a) Insist on splitting it—it's only fair!
b) Ask if you can leave the tip.
c) Graciously let him get it.

On the first date, the guy should always pay (let's hope, anyway!), including tip. It's not a moral imperative but rather standard protocol. Maybe when we stop earning just 76 cents on the dollar compared to men, that will change, but even then, this is a tradition that appears to be sticking around. So enjoy it! A lot of my clients ask if they need to at least offer or do the fake-out wallet reach. You don't. Just let him pick it up and give a genuine

---

FAQ

Q: What if we go out to dinner and my steak is overcooked? Can I send it back?

A: If you're with friends or someone you've been dating for a few months, go ahead, but on a first date, you have to remember that he's reading your every move. If you send back your dinner, odds are that he'll think you'll do it all the time. That's not something you want him to think. Best not to appear hard-to-please on the first date.

---

thank you. Let him know you appreciate it, but there's no need to say something like, "I'll get it next time." First, you're assuming there will be a next time, and second, you don't "owe" him, no matter how much he spent or how grateful you are.

NOW WHAT?

A lot of my clients ask how long they have to sit there if they don't like a guy. First, I ask them to make sure they don't like him. If you're contemplating whether you want to see him again, you should do everything you can to try for a second date. Some of my clients have had situations where they weren't crazy about a guy on a first date, but thought he was a great catch on the second. But for those cases when you absolutely know for certain that you'd rather eat your wineglass than have another drink with him, by all means, end the date. Whether it's a personality clash or a physical one, there's nothing wrong with ending a date early if you know he's not for you. There have been plenty of guys who haven't liked you, too (hard fact to realize, but c'mon, it happens to everyone). That's just the nature of dating.

Advice from Dan Aferiat, Your On-Call Therapist

People always say that when you meet the One, you "just know." Should you keep going out with a guy if you don't have that feeling?

I tell my patients when they date that they don't have to make any decisions about the man unless they are completely repulsed. It's very important to let yourself be confused. There are so many feelings and thoughts rushing through both of your minds in the early stages of dating, and the best tool to help sort them out is time. The guy you're dating is also likely to be feeling confused and pressured. While women are often wondering if he is "the One," men are often wondering if they are good enough to be "the One." They're stepping into a new role that can be unfamiliar and makes them feel very out of control and ashamed. Generally, men are socialized more around physical behavior than emotions, so they are good at having a poker face and not letting women know they may feel vulnerable or interested in investing in a relationship. They may try to protect themselves by continuing to bounce around aimlessly as a bachelor rather than show their cards. And they may not even be aware that they are doing this.

"GIVE THE GUY A CHANCE"
IS DISCRIMINATION AGAINST
SINGLE PEOPLE

Spending forty-five minutes to an hour with a guy is plenty of time to give him a chance. Going so far as accepting a second date—or even a second drink—from someone you're not even remotely interested in is pointless. You know when your friends tell you, "Oh, you should give the guy a chance"? That's what I call discrimination against single people. Just because you are single, doesn't mean you can't have preferences. Tune into your instincts and learn to trust them. Here's a simple test if you want to be sure: Ask yourself which you'd rather do next Saturday night—rent a movie by yourself or endure the company of this guy, who has smoker's breath, whines nonstop about his job, and still lives with his parents. You don't have to settle! If you are genuinely unsure, that's a different story, but you are allowed to dislike someone you don't have chemistry with. If you were hiring someone for a job, you'd want to give all applicants a fair chance. But this is a date. It's all about personal preference.

HOW TO END IT

After that last sip of your pinot grigio, you smile and say, "Well, it was great to meet you/see you again. Thank you so much, but I've got to get going." Although you may feel like you need an excuse to leave, you don't. He shouldn't give you the third degree, but you can always say you're meeting some friends for dinner, should he beg you to stay. If he tries to set up a second date, it's best not to tell him that he must be on crack if he thinks you like him. No need to embarrass the guy in public. Just be vague and leave it up in the air as to when you would go out with him again. If he calls, you can either avoid the phone call or tell him that you don't see any romantic potential. Yes, it sucks to have to reject someone, but he'll live. You don't have time for guilt dates with guys you don't like.

HOT STUFF!

Okay, so what happens when you think he's Brad Pitt, Ben Affleck, and Johnny Depp all rolled into one (or at the very least a quite charming David Schwimmer)? Chances are, the date won't end just because you had only planned on drinks. Let's hope he picks a bar with a restaurant, knowing you can move on to dinner if all goes well. But if he doesn't ask if you want to take a look at a menu, don't push it by saying you're starving and "Oh, is that a free table over there?" He may not be feeling the same vibes you are, or he may opt to take you out again another night instead. Don't put him in the uncomfortable position of saying no. That should be your job. ☺

Some of my clients will ask if they should decline extending a date, because they think that leaving sooner rather than later will make the guy want them all the more. To which I answer: nope! Accepting his invitation trumps hard-to-get, at least in this scenario. He wants to get to know you more and likes your company—nothing wrong with that. Still, be sure to set some boundaries for yourself. Don't go dancing until 3 a.m. on a weeknight, and don't make out for four hours. End the night respectably and at a decent hour. If all goes well, you'll see him again, so no need to cram all your fun into one night!

ALWAYS KISS ON THE FIRST DATE

I say always kiss on the first date, if you like the guy. This is the #1 way to increase your odds of getting to the second date. If you like a guy, it's important to show him. A lot of guys today, whether it's out of shyness or because they're being overly polite, won't even try to make a move on the first date. That can be a positive thing, because it often means he's a good guy and he's in relationship mode. But then it's your job to show him your sexier side and that you're interested in him. When he leans in to say good night, you

> *How many bacteria colonies are exchanged during an average kiss? Answer: 278.*
>
> **Fun Fact**

should go for a passionate kiss. That way, you can both see if there's chemistry, so you're not guessing whether there was or there wasn't after you go your separate ways.

Men get very nervous toward the end of a date and they often won't make the first move unless they know that they won't be rejected. They also won't know that you are sexual unless you show it with your actions. I'm not saying you should maul him. Just wait until he leans in to say good-bye, which most guys will do with a kiss on the cheek, and then give him your lips instead. It is a mutual process at that point. You basically want to make it very easy for him to be able to kiss you. One client of mine was being driven home after a first date, and when they said good night, she kept her seat belt on. She wasn't even able to lean in halfway, which gave him the impression that she wasn't interested in a kiss (in fact, by keeping that seat belt on, it would seem she was scared of one). He awkwardly just said good night. Thankfully, she managed to get another date with him. This time, she took her seat belt off when they got to her house. He did the same, reading that she was giving him a much better signal.

As for how long you should kiss, regardless of who initiates it, that all depends on the kiss. You'll know when things are going too far. There's "I want to see you again" kissing, and then there's "I just want to bang you!" kissing. You've got to pull yourself away if things escalate to groping. Just give him a taste. It's kind of like drug dealers who give away free samples to get someone hooked. Give him just enough that he's going to want to come back for more. Give too much (i.e., go back to his place) and he may not come back, at least not for the reason you want.

While we're on the subject, the end of the date is usually the best time for a kiss. If he tries to plant one on you earlier than that, make it short and sweet. If he pushes for more, you should question what this guy is after: sex or a relationship. A quick one isn't going to hurt earlier on in the date. (Sometimes it can even help break the tension.) But save more serious smooching for the end of the date.

If a guy is pushing you further than you want to go, don't feel bad or guilty about saying no. You don't need to explain yourself or make excuses. "No!" is a whole sentence. If you're interested in the guy, and you get the sense that he is in relationship mode, not sex mode, show him that you are tempted, so he knows that he has a shot next time, but don't give in. Explain that you want to, but not on the first date. Be firm. He'll respect that you have boundaries that you stick to. If his boundaries are a little blurry, he'll especially rely on you to have firm boundaries, even if he seems to be trying to convince you otherwise.

PARTING NOTES

The first date is all about how it ends. A lot of women talk about having a great connection with a guy and having so much to talk about, but remember that actions speak louder than words. If you just wave or hug in front of the bar, or he doesn't at least offer to walk you to your car or a cab, that's not a good sign. Handshake? Terrible. Kiss on the cheek? A little better, but hard to read. A kiss with some passion behind it is a good bet. But how do you really know? You don't. Just relax and wait. If you had good chemistry throughout the date, you kept things breezy and fun, you've got a good chance. Just don't get too caught up in fantasies of this guy being the One. Remember the 1 in 10 rule. If you've never met the guy before, only 1 out of 10 first dates is going to lead to a second date. You may find that statistic discouraging, but it's actually a good thing. The more you go out with guys who aren't a good fit for you, the more you'll be able to detect who *will* be a good fit. Plus, it makes it all the more exciting when something does hold promise. If a guy who is not right for you doesn't call, he's actually doing you a favor. He's not wasting your time. If you felt like the date was going well, and he abruptly ended it, try to examine why once you've parted ways. Don't confront him in this situation. Ask yourself if you dominated the conversation and didn't ask him enough about himself. Or maybe you were pushy about where to go or picky about how you wanted your martini made (translation: high maintenance!).

Still, there's no need to beat yourself up or get obsessive. You might not have done anything wrong. Sometimes, it's just not a match—like the two pieces of the puzzle not fitting together. Just pick up and move on and try to glean some pointers for the next time.

WHEN IS HE GOING TO CALL?!

Now is the hard part. It's awful enduring the agony of waiting for a guy to call, but that's just part of the game. Besides, if you didn't turn the guy into Prince Charming in your head and pin all your hopes and dreams on him, you'll get over it because a) He's not the last guy on earth, as you've noticed from your 15-hour-a-week search; b) If he didn't think you were a good fit together, there's no point in analyzing it; and c) You've got a date lined up for next week already (right?).

THE BIG NO-NO

Do not call him after the date. Not three hours later, not three days later, not three weeks later. Well, by three weeks later you have nothing to lose, but keep in mind that it's a long shot. And no "thank you" e-mail, either. Or one of those "I had a great time" follow-up voice mail messages. You may insist you're simply being nice, but we all know what you're really up to—him included. You're trying to control the situation because the

---

FAQ

Q: But what if he doesn't know I like him?

A: If you flirted and were responsive and if you kissed him back when he went in for the kill, he knows you like him. If you didn't, go back and read this chapter again and improve your first-date skills. You had the whole date to show him that you like him.

waiting is so hard. It's terribly uncomfortable not having any control over a guy calling you back and there's some relief in "doing all you could," but do yourself a favor and don't. Guys do what they want to do. If he is interested, he'll call.

Doing "all you can" to show him you like him after the date can scare him. It can also seem controlling or demanding. Be a little hard to get in order to come across as desirable and confident. By calling him, you're forcing his hand. Now you'll never know whether or not he was going to call you back and when. You won't get to "find out what kind of man he is," and you're left more in the dark than you were before. Unless you always want to be the one doing all the calling, it's wise to let him initiate. Again, think of that tennis game. He's got to be the one who serves. Most women like to be pursued. If you want him to pursue you, then you can't be the initiator.

MEN DON'T HAVE THE ANSWERS

Some of my clients ask me if it's okay to call failed dates later just to see what went wrong. "I need to know!" they say. "Too bad," I say. If there's nothing you can think of that you may have done to ruin the chances of a second date, then let it go. There is no point in asking the guy. You're giving him too much power, first of all. If he says he didn't like your nose, what are you going to do? Go get surgery to fix it? Perhaps he was seeing someone else and it got more serious, or maybe he's in sex mode and doesn't have any interest in changing. Whatever it is, he probably won't tell you the true reason anyway. Oftentimes he doesn't even know. As much as we'd like to think they do, guys don't have all the answers. Chances are, you're putting a lot more time into analyzing the situation than he is. In the way that he understands it, he probably just didn't feel like calling you. Or—the hard truth here—perhaps he didn't like you. It happens; it doesn't mean you did anything wrong. You've certainly had times when you thought someone wasn't a good fit with you, so just let it go and keep your eye on the prize, which is a guy who *does* think you're a good fit. He's out there—you just haven't found him yet.

HE CALLED!

Congratulations! That's awesome. Men don't initiate second dates unless they really want to, so if he called, he's interested. Actions say more than words, and his picking up the phone speaks volumes. (And isn't it so much more gratifying than if you had called him?) In getting asked out again by him, you have passed the threshold that 90% of first dates don't pass. If your hit rate for a guy calling after the first

> **Quick Tip**
>
> *Talk softly. It's sexier. That doesn't mean he should be straining to hear you, but he shouldn't be holding the phone a foot from his ear, either. Take deep breaths before answering the phone. And practice speaking while expelling air. It prevents that nervous tight-throated feeling that can make you sound like Kermit.*

date is higher than 10% (during my peak, I got to about 80%), then you are doing a great job of having your Cablight on! Don't worry about playing it too cool when he calls, either. There's no need to pretend you don't recognize his voice or that you're not home. Best thing to do after he says, "Hi, it's so-and-so . . ." is to say, "Hey, I was just thinking of you." A guy loves to know that he is on your mind. By using that line, you're making him more comfortable and showing that you're interested. And he knows you're not so obsessed or such a control freak that you had to call him.

SECOND- AND THIRD-DATE TIPS

Make yourself available if you like the guy. That doesn't mean that you can't have one night that you are busy, but be sure to have a few times available and don't be too inflexible with your schedule. If he took a long time to call, your first instinct may be to "punish" him by making things tough for him or by acting indifferent or even rude. Fight that urge. I had one client who went on a date with a guy and he didn't call her for two months. The reason was that he had some loose ends to tie up with a past relationship and he wanted to do so before getting involved again. He ended up being a great boyfriend. Bottom line: If he calls (no matter when it is), that's a good thing. But whether he does or he doesn't, keep on truckin'! There are a lot of other men out there who *are* going to call after a date to ask you for another. This is a trial-and-error process, and it's bound to get frustrating at times. But as you go along, stay positive by thinking of dating as a game that you're improving as you go. Each time you go out, imagine it as a practice run for when you meet the right guy for you. He's right around the corner . . . you just have to keep looking.

10

Do What Works

So, are you getting the hang of it yet? Now that you've learned the moves, it becomes a matter of lather, rinse, repeat. The more you date—once a week, right?—the better you're going to be at it. By now, you can probably "name that tune" in fewer notes. You no longer need to go out with a guy five or six times before deciding if you like him or not. In fact, you can probably rule out 80% of guys on the first date because your instincts are getting sharper and sharper. You're probably also learning what works for you in your 15-hours-per-week search, too. Part of my weekly Strategy with my clients is going over what's worked for them and what hasn't in that week's search. Often, they'll start to see patterns in what's been effective for them. They'll discover things like, "Well, when I give my card to guys when they don't ask for it, I don't often get a call. But when I figure out a way to get *them* to ask for it, I usually do get a call!" There's going to be some trial and error, nonetheless. Maybe you're the rare girl who can hand out her card without being asked for it because you do it in a nonaggressive way, or because you happen to like shy guys. That's the difference between dating with a set of Rules vs. dating with my Strategy.

You need to develop your own sense of success. You can ask yourself, "What would Nancy do?" But the idea is that you start to internalize my voice in your head by applying these principles and seeing what works. If you see that something works—whether it's always having great luck at one bar over another, or there's a line you use that always gets a guy's interest—keep doing it! Don't argue with what works, even if you're surprised at what works. If you're having fun, that's a good indication of something working. If you're getting results, that's even better. I want you to stick to the Program, though. This isn't an excuse to drop an aspect you don't like—online dating, for instance—just because you find you're having more success at another aspect, like meeting guys at bars. If you find that your hit rate with online dating isn't great, go back and reread chapter eight and try to figure out what you can improve on and how to have more fun at it. Before you decide to tweak your individual game plan, you need to follow the basics of my Program for a few months and see how it goes. Then you can get creative by putting your own spin on it.

CRITIQUE YOUR GAME

One client of mine who was looking for a relationship gave herself the homework of having a fling to revitalize herself. (Hey, good sex can give a girl a new outlook—more on that in the next chapter!) She expected just to have sex with the guy and end the encounter that night, but he kept calling her and asking her out. Now, I wouldn't advise you to try finding a relationship by way of a one-night stand, but she and I went over what else she did differently with this guy *besides* sleeping with him within hours of meeting him. She realized she'd had a much different attitude with him than she'd had with men she wanted to date. She didn't hang on his every word, didn't censor her own words—she even wore a sexier outfit than she normally would with men she was looking to marry. When a girl is only after a relationship, men can smell it. The fact that she wasn't looking for something long-term had the advantage of putting the guy at ease. Turned out she wasn't interested in Mr. Fling even though he was calling her, but she started using the same tactics with other guys and ended up getting a better hit rate with them. Sometimes it's a good idea to do what you'd do if you didn't care (the same way it works when you go out with sweats and no makeup on and that's the day you get asked out).

Now, notice that I didn't let her go for the obvious answer of "Well, sleeping with a guy on the first date must work for me." You need to look for the deeper and more strategic answer, which is: "I didn't act like a needy, clingy nut with him." It's along the same lines of having a "lucky" pair of jeans. Every time you wear them, you meet a guy. Know that it's probably because you have a different attitude when you're in them—who doesn't feel sexy when their ass looks great?!—not that the denim has been anointed by the Goddess of Dating. (Keep wearing them, though!)

While you're busy figuring out what does work, you should also be figuring out what doesn't work and how you can change that. There's a great *Seinfeld* episode where George decides that his life isn't what he wants, so he starts doing the opposite of everything he'd ever done. And it works! I'm sure you're not quite as off the mark as he was in life, but it might help to switch up some of your routine if certain things aren't working for you. You can't totally avoid wasted time or heartache. Dating is an inefficient process by nature. But you can have some control. For instance, you can't control if a guy is going to call you or not. But you can increase your chances by playing out a good strategy (like wearing those lucky jeans).

TENSION-RELIEVING VS. GOAL-ACHIEVING

It's going to be tempting at times to go against the Strategy I'm teaching, and fall back to what's comfortable for you. The biggest challenge my clients have is to stop trying to control the process. This can sometimes manifest itself in tension relief. If you feel out of control, which you will a lot of the time in dating, there's a lot of tension that you're going to want to relieve. There are two types of actions you can take—tension-relieving or goal-achieving. Doing what comes easy often falls under tension-relieving. For example, when you pick up the phone to "check in" with a guy or e-mail him to find out the movie time: Is the purpose of this goal-achieving or tension-relieving? You

Tension-Relieving	Goal-Achieving
Forwarding him every joke e-mail you receive	Forwarding him directions to the party you're going to together
Burning him a mixed CD	Lending him a CD he asked to borrow
Hanging around his neighborhood to "accidentally" run into him	Going to his neighborhood because your favorite deli is there, then going home!
Calling him (yet again) to check where the restaurant is	Calling the restaurant to see where it is!

don't need to check in with him, and you can look up the movie time in the paper if you really don't remember. Another case of tension-relieving behavior would be if a guy hasn't called you and the ball's in his court and you think, "Well, maybe I'll call again just in case he didn't get the message." If, however, you just got a new phone number and he has no way of reaching you unless you leave it for him, that's goal-achieving. Don't delude yourself, either. Say you have a decision to make about how to spend your 15 hours and you think, "Well, I could go to this party where I don't know anyone . . . or I could do more online dating because it's easier." If you're using online dating as a crutch in this Program and you're not pushing yourself to do other things, like go to parties and events, that is not goal-achieving. So, quit it!

CHILL OUT

I promised you something in this book—that you can find the right guy. I firmly believe that it's within your power if you follow my Program and practice these strategies. But you have to believe it, too. Maybe you've been going out on a date a week and keeping up with your 15 hours a week for a month by now and that feels like a long time for you. "Yeah! That's sixty hours!" you say. But now is just when you're starting to get really good at it, so just relax. It is going to happen. However, there is always some element of luck and fate coming into play. If you're really desperate about exactly when it's going to happen, you're going to lose that playful attitude you need to make this Program work for you. If you obsess about marriage too much, your anxiety might interfere with achieving your goal. Let things evolve naturally, and eventually fate and all your hard work will collide and everything you've been hoping for will finally happen. Whatever you do, don't give up after just dabbling in this. It will get hard at times and you'll wonder if it's ever going to happen, but it will—I promise! Just don't give up. If you use my winning Strategy, you *will* find your dream guy in 6 months or less.

The key to success is to take things one step at a time. Ask yourself if you'd like to have a *drink* with the guy you've just met before you start naming the kids you're going to have together. You know how men supposedly think of sex every eleven seconds or so? Well, a lot of women seem to think about marriage about every eleven seconds. If that's you, don't do that! It's not a good idea to get ahead of yourself. You just want to go with the flow. You'll see where you're going once you get there. One client of mine went out with a guy who lived an hour and a half away, which she thought might be complicated. So, instead of simply seeing if they enjoyed each other's company on their first date and worrying about logistics later, she put him on the spot by saying, "So how do you see this working, given that we live so far apart?" She was worried about how often they'd see each other before even finding out if they *wanted* to see each other! Whether he didn't ask her out again because he didn't think they had enough in common, or because she got too ahead of herself, we'll never know.

You don't want to forget your goal, of course. You probably do want to get married to someone someday, but see if you fit with him first before you fit him for the tux. Once you're committed to this Program, you're covered anyway. If you have your Cablight on and you're spending 15 hours per week on the search and going out on one date per week, then you can relax knowing that you are doing all you can. A guy's biggest fear is that a woman has a one-track mind and is only after him for one thing. And no, it's not sex. It's marriage. Men fear that women are just trying to rope them into the role of husband, without

The Litmus Test

Some questions to ask yourself when you're pondering a guy's worth—and their not-so-useful counterparts:

Good Questions	Bad Questions
Is he fun to hang out with?	Will my mother like him?
Can I see myself going to dinner with him again?	Can I see myself walking down the aisle with him?
Is he a good kisser?	What will we name our children?
Do we have a lot to talk about?	Do we have the same taste in engagement rings?
Do I like seeing his name on my Caller ID?	Do I like how my first name sounds with his last name?

regard for them as people. It's true that men can smell desperation, so if you can't show you have anything to give in return, they'll just see you as trying to squeeze the juice out of them. You have to show him you're pretty juicy yourself first!

ASKING TOO MUCH

Along with planning too far ahead, you don't want to fall into the trap of expecting too much early on in dating. You don't have to be the center of his universe! A lot of women make the assumption that having a relationship means talking every day. If you're starting to see someone and he doesn't call or e-mail every day, that's okay. In fact, it's often better that way. A guy I dated for a while had a great line that made me see the value in not speaking to one another every day. He explained, "I like to miss you." It is nice to have a couple of days of anticipation—it can even be exciting. Gets your heart beating faster when you see each other! Of course, if a guy's pattern is completely sporadic and he's unreliable, that's different. But if

Advice from Dan Aferiat, Your On-Call Therapist

Why aren't men more open with their feelings?

Although the socialization for men and women is different, the internal experience of being alive is largely the same for both sexes. In my opinion, there are not significant gender differences in cravings for human contact, connectedness, or love. But because men in this society are taught that their manhood is judged by their emotional self-control, they are cautious about revealing their feelings. They often achieve emotional closeness with their buddies by watching sports, with the "high-five" representing the hug they deny themselves in order to feel manly. But women have the power to help men feel safe showing their emotions. Knowing that it's okay to cry or admit fears are a couple of examples of how men can learn from the "fairer" sex. Shame is a powerful force that can shut down emotions, but a woman's acceptance can draw them out.

you're seeing each other a couple of times a week, and he's consistent in his interest, there's no need to overdo it.

EMOTIONAL EXPECTATIONS

You might be expecting too much emotionally from the guys you date. Perhaps you think he should be "completing you" and other nonsense. Realize that a relationship doesn't have to mean that you're joined at the hip, you finish each other's sentences, and you do everything together. In fact, those types of relationships tend to crash and burn. Think Billy Bob Thornton and Angelina Jolie. Carrying one another's blood in vials around their necks, getting those ridiculous tattoos, and not being able to take their eyes off each other—or their hands, for that matter—even at public events. They fell victim to a crash-and-burn relationship, in which their mutual adoration was so intense, so addictive, that it wasn't healthy or sustainable.

When you meet someone who's right for you, it's tempting to want to meld as one and never be apart, but you may notice that the more healthy relationships in your life have a degree of separation to them. Separation is also a great way to keep the passion alive. Try to relax and not rush things, even if he's the one being obsessive. In fact, I'd be extra cautious with guys who are extremely intense off the bat (like Billy Bob) be-

> *If you're having a difficult time getting into relationships because you think you and a man should be completing each other, pick up* Getting the Love You Want, *by marriage counselor Harville Hendrix, who says the healthiest relationships are not "symbiotic."*

Quick Tip

cause they're often the ones that disappear the fastest, too. Or at least tend to have commitment issues. (Billy's at five marriages and counting.) If a relationship gets too heated without building a strong foundation first, it's in danger of imploding. These connections are often built more on fantasy than reality.

You don't even have to spend all your time together talking. It's okay just to hang out and watch a movie, or even sit in silence. (Imagine that?!) I know it seems odd, but guys actually like that. Keep in mind that a relationship is more about sharing leisure time than anything else. If he likes having you by his side while watching all four *Lethal Weapon* movies, who's to say that's not as good an indicator of a lasting, meaningful relationship as writing love songs for each other on his and hers harps?

ENVISIONING, WITH FLAWS

When you picture your Mr. Right, what do you see? Often, women imagine a guy who's equal parts handsome, funny, smart, rich, gentlemanly, and generous, who's also great in bed. You can find someone with a lot, if not all, of these qualities. But you have to be realistic, too. You don't want to feel like you're settling, but you may have to give up a few things. Maybe he's not as social as you. Maybe his wallet isn't as thick as Bill Gates's, or his sense of humor isn't quite of Jim Carrey proportions. We all have flaws—even you. I do an exercise with my clients called "envisioning," where they envision the guy they are looking for. Then I tell them to picture the flaws they could live with. Try to think of some shortcomings that you could handle, so you can have a bit more of an open mind. Imagine what you can live with versus what you can't. If you like to clean, then maybe it wouldn't be so bad having a guy who's

Not-So-Acceptable Flaw	Acceptable Flaw
He's cheap.	He buys cheap clothes.
He cheats on you.	He enjoys his porn.
He has no drive.	He has a crummy car.
He lies about his whereabouts.	He lies about liking your mother.
He's an alcoholic.	He gets drunk on poker night.
He never calls.	He never calls during *Monday Night Football.*
He doesn't pay his taxes.	He doesn't pay you compliments 24-7.
He plays mind games.	He plays video games.

messy. If you're a sympathetic listener, then maybe you can handle someone more emotional than you. Maybe it's not such an issue for you if a guy is shorter than you, or if he doesn't have all his hair. A lot of women find men more attractive the more they get to know them, too. Have you ever had an inexplicable crush on a not-so-attractive colleague? Give guys in the dating pool the same kind of chance. At least for one date, anyway. If you've been having a tough time finding guys online that you want to write to, or you quickly dismiss most men who express an interest in you, reconsider next time. You could be missing out on a great catch, just because he doesn't fit your Prince Charming ideal.

If you find you're too attached to that perfect fantasy guy you've always envisioned, you might have more trouble with finding the One. You'll have to let go of your perfectionist standards a little, since nobody's perfect. The key is that you will gain something far more fulfilling as a result—a relationship with a real man.

DEAL-BREAKERS

Of course there are certain qualities you shouldn't compromise on. Does a guy have good character, for instance? That's a little harder to judge, but that's why you take your time getting to know someone. He should also have some ethical or moral standards, which you'll be able to measure more easily as you get to know him. You're allowed to have deal-breakers. Maybe a guy has to be of the same religion as you. That's valid. The three or so things that are most important to you should be your deal-breakers. Just be sure that you have good reasons be-

In My Clients' Words

One guy I started dating was in the process of getting divorced. That was something I could handle. But they were still sharing the house and that became a problem for me. He was so worried about hurting his soon-to-be ex's feelings that he felt he shouldn't go on Saturday night dates while he was still living there, even though they were living in separate rooms and not even speaking anymore. I got fed up pretty quickly and had to end things. —Joanna

hind them. Some women rule a guy out if he is under six feet tall. If you're 5'11", that's understandable. If you're 5'2", you should reconsider.

When Courteney Cox started dating David Arquette, he was using drugs and drinking a lot. Those, to her, were unacceptable habits, and she couldn't date him as long as he was in party mode. He quickly realized she was more valuable to him than that lifestyle, so he quit. She did not, however, insist that he start dressing better. His love for primary-colored suits and test-pattern shirts was a flaw she could accept and even embrace. They even went on to produce a TV show about how couples can decorate combining both their styles.

SEE HIM FOR WHAT HE IS

The poet Maya Angelou has a great saying: "When someone shows you who they are, believe them, the first time." Note that she says *shows* you, not *tells* you. Read his *actions*, not his *words*. Don't believe what you want to believe. If you know you're too trusting with men, give yourself more time with a guy before getting too emotionally attached. While you may not get everything on your list of most-wanted traits, what most women want from a guy is loyalty and the ability to be faithful. Pay attention to the signs that reflect this. Some guys are not capable of being faithful, and that doesn't change easily.

Past actions can be part of it. If you know for a fact that he's cheated on other women—he might even be cheating on someone else with you—he's very likely to do it again. That's part of his character. And that's not good character. If he lies habitually, that's also not good character. Don't be forgiving with things like that! Is he always blatantly checking out other women and comparing you to them? Does he make degrading comments to you? It's not going to come out at first, because most jerky guys know how to mimic a nice guy. Sooner or later, a man's true personality comes out. In the meantime, be a bit of a detective for red flags. There's no point in probing, because if he's up to no good, he'll probably lie, but notice details the way Nancy Drew would and put the clues together. Don't ignore telltale signs.

HAVE GOOD AIM

Just as you don't want to turn down a guy simply because he's got a funny haircut, you don't want to go out with anything that moves, either. Some women will chronically date men who don't have a lot to offer because their self-esteem is low. Aiming for someone they really want, who excites them and challenges them, is a lot scarier than going out with that unemployed pot-head with the credit-card debt. You certainly have less control in the relationship with someone who is your equal, but it's also infinitely more exciting. When people say, "I've met my match," I like to think of it in the boxing sense. You need someone on your level to spar with, otherwise it's no fun. The conflicts in your relationship are going to help make it thrive. Put yourself on the line and seek more challenging partners. You might feel more vulnerable when you are hurt or rejected, but you're also going to be much more fulfilled—and thrilled!

It's sort of like picking apples. The low-hanging fruit may be

> **Quick Tip**
>
> *The best relationships are the ones in which both people feel lucky to have found the other.*

easier to reach, but the higher up, the better the pick. Try to aim as high as you can reach. But know your limits. If you are constantly going for the Calvin Klein–model types when you haven't been to the gym in years, you may be setting yourself up for rejection.

ADVANCED STRATEGIES TO KEEP YOU ON TRACK

Now that you've learned your Dating 101, it's time to graduate to the next class!

Don't Flinch

The night I met my husband I was out at a social function, scoping for men. I saw him and thought he was cute. I wanted to meet him. But I was there alone, and I was shy and embarrassed, so I left. I flinched. Don't do that! Because the thought of taking a chance is so scary, most people's minds, including my own, will give them 20 million reasons not to do something. You're going to talk yourself out of every opportunity if you're not careful. In this case, I got another chance, the very same night! I was lucky. And that second time, I didn't flinch. I felt like fate gave me another chance and I wasn't going to miss it again. If you miss too many chances, you may not get another one. Think of the Nike slogan and "Just do it"!

Your reflexes have to be sharp, especially if you live in a big city. In small towns or at college, you run into the same people over and over again, so you can let a flirtation build over time. But if you eye someone at a bar in a big city, you might never see him again, so you have to make a move—and fast. Don't wait until you've had enough drinks to get up the nerve to approach

him. By then, another girl could have intercepted, and suddenly
he has her phone number instead of yours.

Invest in Stages

There's a temptation to throw everything out there on the first
date. But it's not smart to share all your personal details all at
once, just as it's not smart to sleep with him right away. You invest *slowly*. You need to learn to trust him in stages. Some
women tend to think a guy can be trusted completely or not at
all. There's no gray area, only black and white. They can't deal
with the fact that if he calls Wednesday instead of Tuesday, it
doesn't mean he's untrustworthy. It just means he called late.
Or, an even worse trap, they think that if he does call on time,
he's completely trustworthy. Aim for somewhere between being
too guarded and being too trusting. If you invest slowly, you'll
feel more confident in your investment by the time you do give
him more of your trust and your heart. Dating is a process. It
takes time.

The Winding Road

In your search, you should believe you're going to get from
point A to point B, but it's important that you don't overanalyze
quite how you're going to get there. When I was a headhunter, I
would call companies having no idea if they had a job available
to list with me. Oftentimes they didn't, but then in the course
of talking, they'd refer me to another company that did need
my service. So even if you're absolutely certain something won't
work, keep that spirit of always giving it a shot. You might even
have to go out of your way sometimes. When I was single, I had
nothing better to do than follow a guy that I liked. I didn't care

if people knew I had nothing better to do. Learn to follow your destiny without having an agenda.

Be the Constant

I've told you before that dating is an out-of-control process by nature, but that you do have some control. Here's how you can increase your level of control: Try thinking of dating as a scientific experiment where there's a constant and a variable. You should always be the constant. Being consistent in your approach will help you judge guys better. If you're both variable, the study won't make sense! If your behavior follows a set pattern, you will have an easier time finding out what kind of man *he* is. For example, on the first date, say you kiss every guy you go out with good night, but you stop things from going any further, and they all seem fine with that. Then suddenly there's one guy who suggests you're a big tease. You can feel very safe in knowing this guy's a jerk and that you weren't a tease, because he's the only guy who thought that. But let's say you've acted differently with every guy you've been out with. Maybe you were overly touchy with some guys, you slept with others, and you didn't even give a handshake to some. Then you'll be less sure what signals you might have sent this guy throughout the night and you might question whether you are, in fact, acting like a tease. Keep your actions fairly consistent, and you'll get a better read on the guys you go out with. You can't find out what kind of man he is if you're always changing.

You're Only Looking for One

Occasionally, a client will tell me: "I only meet losers at singles events." I always say that if they have an option to go to something better, where "cooler" relationship-seeking singles might be loitering in the same numbers as at a singles event, then go. But don't rule out events because you think most of the people won't be for you. You don't need "most of the people"—you just need one. Who's to say there isn't a guy there who got dragged by his friends, who might want to snicker in a corner with you about how everyone else is a loser? Just give it a shot. One of my clients, who is in her early thirties, went to a singles event, and when she walked in the door, she immediately noticed that all the guys looked to be over 60. She was ready to bag it, but she pushed herself to stay. She soon noticed the one guy who happened to be around her age. They quickly sought each other out and ended up dating.

Run for the Subway

New York City is great for people-watching, and one thing that I've noticed is that everyone always runs to catch the bus when they see it, no matter how far they are from it. But they don't run down the street to the subway station in the hopes that their train is there, even if they're late. I've often pondered why that is. The reason is that they can't see the train coming, so they don't assume it's there. When you're single, it's hard to picture being in a great relationship. But if you envision it and run for it, you will be more likely to catch it. Visualize that relationship being right around the corner, and if you don't hustle, you're going to miss it! Have a sense of urgency in your search and really try to make it happen. Your man could be just around the corner.

You Vote with Your Feet

When my clients are trying to figure out if they like a guy or not, I tell them my dad always says, "You vote with your feet."

What that means is that a lot of the time your actions reflect how you're feeling. It's the same principle as reading a guy's actions, not his words. If a guy calls you and leaves a message and you forget to call him back, you've pretty much answered your own question. On the other hand, if the phone rings and you

I dated this guy for two months, but I was never that excited about going out with him. We met each other's parents and friends, but it all seemed like such a halfhearted attempt on my part. I noticed I started to take longer and longer to return his calls, and then I just stopped altogether. I guess I liked the idea of Tom, but I wasn't that into Tom. —Anna

In My Clients' Words

have to hold yourself back from picking up on the first ring, in hopes that it's him, you're obviously interested. Learn how to read your own actions just as you would read a guy's actions.

THE BREAKUP TALK

Yep, breaking up sucks, but whether you're the one being dumped or you're the one doing the dumping, there's a way to get past it, over it, and on to the next thing. If it's been one or two dates, you can just not return his calls. (Yes, I'm letting you off the hook.) Three or four dates, you should tell him. The phone is okay, and no big explanation necessary. But if it's been one or two months? You should probably do it in person. I know the temptation is to avoid confrontation by taking the easy way out with a text message (*U R 2 old 4 me!*) or maybe on a Post-it, like Berger did to Carrie on *Sex and the City*, but try to do what you'd want if he were the one doing the dumping. Think of breaking up with someone, rather than simply avoiding them, as character-building for you. You might have issues about being rejected, so you're reluctant to do it to someone else, but you need to learn to do it in order to grow. Learning confrontation skills will help you get into a healthy relationship. One of my clients would just keep going out with guys instead of breaking up with them because she felt so sorry for them. I said to her, "Who's going to feel sorry for you?" That question really stuck with her.

When breaking up with a guy, avoid making it too personal. The last thing you want to do is go over all his faults. If you're breaking up with someone who doesn't want to break up with you, he's going to try to convince you that he's not the loser or jerk you seem to think he is. There is also no need to get petty with him, unless he has truly wronged you in some way. Be clear, be confident, and be firm. "It doesn't feel right for me" usually works really well, or "I know myself and I just don't feel it's a fit." How can he argue with what you're feeling? Sure, he might be upset, but it's going to be much better if you do it swiftly than if you drag it out. (Did you know that a wound from a sharp knife heals much faster than one from a dull knife?) If you say something wishy-washy like, "I can't tell if this is going anywhere . . ." and open the topic up for debate, he may try to convince you to give it more time. What's the point if you know you don't like him?

If he breaks up with you, I want you to realize it's not really personal to you, either. You really have to believe that he's doing you a favor. He's obviously not right for you if he's breaking up with you. You have to believe him when he says you're not a good fit. It's his prerogative to make this decision, just as it is yours. Don't try to convince him otherwise, either. You can't make someone like you. You just have to accept it. Show some grace and dignity by simply saying, "I wish you didn't feel that way, but I have to respect your feelings. Call me if anything changes." Let him make the break easily, and you never know, he might come back down the road. Guys often do. Just don't sit around waiting for him or use that as an excuse to not get back in the Program! There's always another guy right around the corner.

The less afraid you are of breaking up and moving on, the less painful it becomes. The more practiced you are at starting and ending relationships—whether they last one weekend or one year—the more easily you can bounce back. And the better you'll be at dating overall. One client of mine got ditched after sleeping with a guy. He called her two days after they spent the night together and said he'd gotten back together with an ex-girlfriend. So how did she recover? She got right back on that dating horse. "I was like, 'Screw this! I'm not letting that guy upset me!'" she said. She was experienced enough in my Program to know that the more dates you have (remember the one date per week quota) the less mission-critical each one will be. You will become more relaxed, and you'll have more success.

That's why you need to stick to this Program over a long period of time, especially if you're relatively new at the dating game. If this is the first time in your life you're dating this intensively, you almost don't want to meet someone right away because you might choose the wrong guy. It's important to develop a basis of comparison. You'll have a better understanding of what you're looking for and be able stand up for what you want. Those qualities aren't just going to help you in dating. They're going to help you in long-term relationships, as well.

SHAKE IT OFF

If you're just coming off a breakup and it hurts, try not to dwell on your sorrow. Think of Kerri Strug at the 1996 Olympics

In My Clients' Words

The toughest part of this Program is finding something in yourself that can keep pressing forward when it's hard. But you keep doing it because that's just what you have to do. Like a job or anything else you have to work hard at to be good at, it requires commitment. —Dana

and how her coach Bela Karolyi told her, "Shake it off!" after she tore two ligaments in her ankle. She had to go back on that vault and guarantee that gold. Of course you can be sad, but not for days on end. One guy's take on your potential for a future together really has no correlation to your ability to find someone else. If you connected with him, even if he's not the One, that says you're getting better at dating and the guy who *is* going to go the distance with you is closer than you think. As they say in sales, "Every no leads you closer to a yes."

PUSH PAST YOUR COMFORT ZONE

I know this process is going to be hard sometimes. But you have to do it anyway. Keep up with your 15 hours and don't stop going on a date a week until you meet the right guy for you. It will happen, but only if you make the effort. You can't do this Program halfway and expect it to work. And you can't give up before the 6 months are up, just because you feel like it's too hard. The payoff for sticking with it is way too huge! And the alternative is way too lonely.

I like to look at this Program almost as a workout program. You know when you're doing push-ups and you just can't do anymore? Then your trainer or your buddy tells you to do just two more. You might think there's no way you can do it, but you push yourself and guess what? You do! Challenge yourself to talk to that guy sitting next to you on the subway or the guy you keep running into at the dry cleaners. Push past your comfort zone, and you're going to get amazing results. A lot of fears come up in dating. Fear of rejection is one that is especially hard to take. It's going to be painful at times to push yourself the way I've asked you to. But do it anyway. This is also why it can help to have a coach. A coach can push you past what you think your limits are much better than you can. If you find that you would benefit from that motivation, get in touch with me for some one-on-one coaching. I love to help. It can be really hard to do alone. So you don't have to be alone! Just don't give up.

11

Sex!

The thing that is foremost on guys' minds (and should be on your mind) after a few dates is sex. Which brings up the age-old question: "When do we *do it*?!" At one of my seminars on dating, a woman asked it this way: "I know that men usually expect sex by the third date, and I'm not usually comfortable until the tenth date, so where's the middle ground?" I answered, "How 'bout six and a half?" The fact is, there *is* a middle ground, yet a lot of women get caught up in the power struggle over sex. In other words, they don't want to "give it up" to the men on their terms, so they hold off altogether, despite themselves. Sex is too often thought of as something men always want and women always deny them. I want you to get that out of your head right now, because, above all, sex should be FUN! It's something you should *both* want and enjoy. Still, there is a negotiation going on that you need to understand before you go forward.

SEX AND EXCLUSIVITY

The biggest mistake women make when it comes to sex is thinking it will bring the relationship to a whole new level. They believe that if they have sex with a guy, it clinches the deal. Women tend to equate sex with being in an exclusive relationship, but exclusivity should never be assumed. The status of your relationship depends more on what you've established outside the bedroom. For instance, if he's not calling you every day, it's certainly not a given that he's going to call the day after you have sex. If you're the type, and most women are, who wants to get a call the next day from a guy you sleep with, and you're going to be upset if you don't, or if you need to know you're the only girl he's seeing, wait until that status has been established. The more dates you have with him, the more proof you're going to have of what kind of man he is. The fewer dates you have, the more of a gamble you're taking. This is not to say that you should hold off to prove a point, but rather that you should be sure you are emotionally ready to handle sex.

SEX AND THE SEXES

I know there are exceptions, but in general, men and women think very differently about sex, and they react to it differently, too. While men can be more removed, women tend to be affected by the act on an emotional level as well as a physical one. It makes sense to me, for instance, that if you sleep with someone and enjoy it, you want to do it again with that person. But men don't always feel the same way. Whether it's the "thrill of the chase" or that they're hardwired to sow their seed, there are some guys who will disappear after the conquest. These are the ones in sex mode. Not all guys will do this, but it is hard to know the difference. This is why, if you're not willing to take the risk that he'll disappear on you after you have sex, you should hold out for a stronger connection *before* you do it rather than relying on it coming along *after.*

Men aren't thinking about marriage and babies and what

you're going to register for at Williams-Sonoma when they're in bed with you. Of course, you may not be thinking that far ahead, either, but chances are, you're thinking more long-term than the guy is. If you take the premise that men are just like women and are thinking the same way as you when you have sex, you're going to have a bad strategy. It's sometimes painful to think that a guy might not be as consumed with emotions as you are, especially your first time together. But no matter how powerful either of your orgasms are, when he's in the moment, he's not picturing himself proposing. That doesn't mean he's using you or that he's callous. And it's not that your own feelings aren't valid. It simply means that sex is different for him.

HOW TO SAY NO

So what do you do when you're all hot and bothered but you're worried that he'll split faster than you can say, "I like my coffee black" if you do spend the night with him? You can say no. When and how you say no to a guy is extremely important, though. If you wait until you're caught up in the moment and nearly at the point of no return to tell him you want to take things slow, that's not a winning strategy. Your boundaries aren't going to be made clear if, at the time you set them up, you're in the heat of passion and possibly both a little tipsy. One time when I was single, I was fooling around with a guy I had just started dating and told him I wanted to "take things slow." He said, "I don't know what that means. Minutes? Or hours?" I actually meant weeks or months. Communication needs to be very clear when it comes to saying no or you risk being pressured—or worse, pushed—into sex. And the more of a jerk you suspect he could be, the more cautious you should be. Even if you're certain your guy is in relationship mode, that doesn't

---

Top Five *Ineffective* Ways of Saying No

5. "Oh, gee, I dunno. I kinda have to get up early. . . . Wow, that feels good . . ."
4. "Okay, I'll spend the night, but we have to keep our clothes on."
3. "Pour me another drink and I'll see how I feel."
2. "Gosh, my bra feels tight. Would you mind if I took it off?"
1. "Oh, yes!"

---

mean he's not going to try for sex if he thinks he's got the opportunity. He's caught up in the moment, too, and when he's at full mast, his judgment might not be what it should be.

SET YOUR BOUNDARIES

If you feel like you need to be explicit about why you want to wait, set your boundaries earlier in the evening, especially when you anticipate being tempted later on. If, say, things got intense on your last date and you think he's going to "expect" sex on this date, but you're not ready, bring it up with him on your way home from dinner. It doesn't have to be a big dramatic conversation. All you say is, "I know things got pretty heated the other night, which was really fun, but I'm not ready for things to go much further." Another way to put this is, "I only have sex when I'm in an exclusive relationship, and I don't think we're there yet." Then drop it. You've made your boundaries clear without being needy or pushy, but you've also put the ball in his court. It puts you in a vulnerable position, but better to feel vulnerable before you have sex than after.

You may risk scaring him if you use the "R" word, but if he's not going to be accommodating to your rather reasonable request, so be it—onward and upward for you. You have to follow through, though. No reneging on the promise you made to yourself and the line you've drawn for him. Not only will he not respect you; he'll think you don't respect yourself. Plus, if you cross your own boundaries, he'll never take your boundaries very seriously in the future. Remember that the reason you might want to wait is not for the purpose of dangling sex like a carrot in front of him, using it to make him want you more. The wait is in order to see what kind of guy he is before you do something that might be too much for you to handle. Waiting is for your benefit more than his. But if he's in relationship mode, then he will respect, even embrace, your boundaries. He will want to take it slow, and he'll expect you to be the one to set limits. Often, it's a relief for him when you say no and slow things down.

Now there is a chance he'll immediately say, "Sure we can be exclusive!" but I wouldn't put much stock into that statement if it's said in reaction to your statement. Don't make the mistake of reading into his words just because they're what you want to hear. If he were to bring up the idea of exclusivity himself at a later date, of his own volition, that's more of an action. He's not simply reacting to something you've said, but stating something he's been thinking about. It's also very important, if you are going to state your boundaries to him, that you not do it in the form of a question. This isn't *Jeopardy!* The last thing you want to do is force him into saying something he might not be feeling by asking, "Are we in an exclusive relationship?" or "How do you feel about seeing each other more often?" or anything else along those lines. That will get you nowhere because you're putting him on the spot, first of all, and not taking his lead. And secondly, there's a chance he could lie just to get in your pants. You know that Meatloaf song, "Paradise by the Dashboard Light"? His date keeps asking him if he'll love her forever and he gets so worked up he finally agrees, but then he ends the song by saying, "Now I'm praying for the end of time . . . so I can end my time with you!" Needless to say, you don't want him saying things he doesn't sincerely mean.

So as to not have a big, often pointless, discussion about both your positions on the matter, like your own weird version of CNN's *Crossfire*, the best thing you can do is change the subject immediately after stating why you want to take your time. Also, you could make your decision to hold off on sex much less daunting for him by saying something like "But we can still have fun . . ." Give him a smile and a passionate kiss and let him imagine what might be in store. You can still explore and enjoy each other's bodies even though you're not going all the way yet. In fact, it's a great way to find out what turns you both on.

DON'T MAKE SEX TOO IMPORTANT

Of course I want you to do what's right for you when it comes to sex, but there's also a chance you're making too big a deal of it. If you're the type who tends to get too attached afterward and who waits an unusually long time before being "ready" for sex, then you should probably teach yourself to chill. Now, I don't want you to get counter-phobic, for example to sleep with a guy on the first date because you feel you should force yourself to handle more. This makes about as much sense as a person with a deathly fear of heights going skydiving. But take a look at the hang-ups you might have about sex. Some of us were brought up to believe that sex is emotionally risky, because it's giving away a part of yourself. I say it's far more risky to give your heart away than your body (as long as you're having protected sex, that is). It's important to allow yourself to get pleasure out of sex, and not to take it *so* seriously. If you make too much of it, you're not only putting too much pressure on yourself, but too much pressure on whomever you're dating, too. It helps not to fantasize about marriage too much in the early stages of dating. It's okay not to be sure if you're headed for the altar before you head for the bedroom. Besides, you need to see if you're even good together sexually. That's a very important part of a marriage, and you want a partner you click with physically. If you're waiting to be absolutely certain that a guy is going to be your husband before you go to bed with him, you're not being realistic. You may have bought this book because you've decided you're done with fooling around and it's time for you to get serious about getting married. But this isn't something that you can completely control or know in advance. You might end up having a few more relationships before you meet Mr. Right. If they hold hope for a future and are healthy and fun, why shouldn't you be having sex? It's part of life. Besides, fooling around is fun. Think of that George Michael song lyric: "Sex is natural . . . sex is good . . . not everybody does it, but everybody should!"

One client of mine met this great guy, and they had instant chemistry, but he was only in the United States on a temporary work visa. Knowing he was only going to be around for a few months, she didn't want to get involved with him, even though she knew the sex would be great. She was shocked when I said to go for it. It's good to have these experiences. Why deprive yourself of fabulous sex and companionship just to save yourself a few days of heartache at the end? Plus, knowing that it couldn't be a long-term romance removed all the expectations and pressure that sometimes go with relationships. She ended up having an amazing time with him and she saw qualities in him that she realized were important to her, including great sexual chemistry. Her standards with other men changed for the better as a result.

TRY BEFORE YOU BUY

Sex is a hugely important part of a relationship, and one you should explore before you get too close in other ways. You can tell a lot about your compatibility with a guy based on your sexual chemistry with him. First of all, there should be some. You should feel those butterflies in your stomach when you're taking each other's clothes off. The sex doesn't have to be completely perfect, like in some Fabio romance novel, but you should click. There should be a connection there, even if it's not quite fine-tuned yet.

You can learn a lot about a guy from his sexual style, too. He should be as into giving as he is into receiving, and hopefully he'll take his time during the act as well as leading up to it. You don't want someone who's going to be selfish and pushy (forcing your head down while you're giving oral sex, for instance), or who isn't going to take any of your needs into consideration. If you've waited a long time to sleep with a guy and you're enamored of him, you might be inclined to accept bad behavior in bed, feeling like you owe it to him at that point. You may think, "Oh, well, he's nice in other ways, so it's okay that he's a one-minute man who doesn't even want to learn what foreplay is." It's not a good idea to make excuses for him when it comes to sex. Read the red flags. On the other hand, you don't necessarily want your guy to be like Don Juan. Frankly, those "know every button to push" guys are usually womanizers. It's better to look for someone who makes you feel good and whom you could make feel good in return. You want to rule out bad behaviors

> ## Essentials in Making Your Apartment Man-Ready
>
> - Mood music—think Alicia Keys, not the Indigo Girls
> - Beer and top-shelf chilled vodka, lime and ice (know how to make a mean martini!)
> - Cool barware
> - Comfy couch—make sure you both sit on it, not in separate chairs
> - Breakfast food—just in case
> - Sexy lingerie (hide the practical bras and granny panties)
> - Condoms
> - Bedroom toys
> - Lack of teddy bears, dolls, or other such items anyone beyond the fourth grade shouldn't have

more than anything and just confirm that there's a good amount of chemistry there. You also want to speak up for what you want in bed. Don't expect him to read your mind.

DON'T WORRY ABOUT YOUR "NUMBER"

Some women, I find, tend to wait too long to have sex or settle for bad sexual chemistry (or both) because they don't want to add to their "number," i.e., their list of men they've slept with. They don't want to go past a certain number of sex partners. But why? Who needs to know your number? It's nobody's business. You're beating yourself up for no reason if you feel guilty about sleeping with more than X number of men. As long as you're using protection, it's okay to sleep with new people and not have it work out. Sex has to be part of your evaluation of a guy and how well he works with you. So instead of thinking of it as icing on the cake, think of it as part of the cake. It's a key ingredient in a relationship and not something you need to compromise on. After all, keep in mind that the man you marry will—presumably—be your sole sex partner. So you should share something good.

FLIPPING A GUY FROM RELATIONSHIP MODE INTO SEX MODE

I'm often asked by clients why sleeping with a guy on the first couple of dates is a bad idea. They wonder: "If you're certain he's looking for a relationship and you seem perfect for each other, what's the harm in going straight to the goods?" First of all, how can you be certain about him so early on? Second, as I've mentioned, he'll actually think *you're* the one in sex mode if you do it too soon. He's not going to assume that your behavior is specific to him. He's not thinking: "Oh, she must really think I'm special if she's sleeping with me." He's thinking you do that with all the guys. And you won't be able to convince him otherwise. He wants you to want to have sex with him, and his machismo will dictate that he has to try to talk you into it, but trust me when I say that if he's a good guy, he really wants you to say no. Even if you somehow get across that you don't sleep with every Tom, Dick, or Harry who buys you dinner— that he's such a special guy, you made an exception—that's a little odd for him to hear. Now he's going to think you consider sex as some gift you're giving to him, and that the only reason you did it was because you see him as marriage material. That's not going to be appealing to him, either. One client of mine ran into a guy who never called her after a first date. I wouldn't advise anyone to do this (she did this *before* she started my Program), but she actually asked him why he never called her again. She hadn't slept with him, but they had discussed sex on the date (one of my no-no's) and she had told him she hadn't had sex in a year and a half. So when she asked him what happened, he said the reason why he didn't ask her for a second date was that she seemed to put too much importance on sex. It's too much pressure for a guy to think you might be looking for him to be the "One" who takes your newfound virginity. When it comes to sex, as with a lot of other aspects of dating,

---

Advice from Dan Aferiat, Your On-Call Therapist

How can you be emotionally prepared for sex for the first time with someone?

Sex intensifies everything. Denying that it means something is not a realistic attitude. Because you don't yet know what sexual intercourse means to the man, literally letting him inside you before you know him is not the most self-protective behavior. I often liken developing closeness with someone to investing in your portfolio. Just as it would not be prudent to put your life savings into a stock without researching it, investing in a man should also require time and research. On the other hand, if you make a decision that you want to have sex with a man without any commitment, be clear with yourself about your intent. Keep in mind that this is not about making a moral judgment, but rather about learning how to take care of your own desires.

find the happy medium. Don't sleep with him on the first date, but don't wait until your fiftieth date, either. Find that middle ground.

Another reason that you don't want to have sex on the first or second date is that for most guys, having sex is a lot easier than having a relationship, so if you get to it too early, they might just decide to quit while they're ahead. Relationships are far more complicated and require obligation and maybe some dreaded "talks about us" that guys might not want to deal with. They might even anticipate you expecting an exclusive relationship now that you have had sex, and, frankly, they don't know you well enough yet to want that themselves. You haven't had enough time to see what kind of man he is. He may not even know what kind of man he is. When you have sex too soon, you're cutting a relationship off at the knees.

FINDING THE BAD BOY IN THE GOOD GUY

I'm sure you've all had a bad boy in your life at some point who was really fun to date. (I hope so, anyway!) But relationship material? Not a good bet. Maybe he was more into partying with his pals than hanging out with you, or his only aspiration in life was tuning up his Harley. He may even have cheated on you, as most true bad boys are not the type to settle down with one woman. But, regardless of the reason things weren't on the path toward marriage, you probably had *wild* sex with him. There's a huge appeal to bad boys. Just look at Tommy Lee. He has drug and alcohol problems, a wicked temper, and has even been to jail for beating his wife, but still, women keep flocking to him, including the one he's been arrested for beating. It's just not smart to seek out relationships with the bad boys. Occasional sex is one thing, but don't delude yourself. They're unreliable, occasionally abusive, often unfaithful, and the great sex and fun you have with them ultimately won't matter compared to the misery they'll put you through in every other aspect of your relationship. You don't want to end up like Mary-Louise Parker, stranded in your seventh month of pregnancy because your so-called boyfriend decides he likes Claire Danes better.

Still, just because your goal should be to find a nice guy to spend the rest of your life with doesn't mean you have to give up the good stuff that bad boys have to offer. In fact, you can use your bad-boy experience to guide you with the good guys. There is a way to get the best of both worlds. It just happens to be easier to find the bad boy in the good guy than to re-form a bad boy.

> *It just feels right dating a good guy. From the first day we met, we were totally at ease with each other. There have been no hidden agendas, no power plays or games, no guarded speech. I have never felt so safe with a man or as cherished. —Judith*

In My Clients' Words

When my clients start working with me, I often discover that they act completely differently around men they might want to marry than around the bad boys in their life. With the bad boy, they might dress a little more provocatively, make a naughty comment here and there, and act more sexual and relaxed in general. With the nice guy, they'll be very reserved, bordering on uptight, in order to show that they're just as straight-laced as they suspect the guy is. The same girl who was doing tequila shots with the guy in the leather jacket the night before will act downright prudish on a date with the guy in the suit and tie. It doesn't have to be this way. The appeal of a bad boy is that he often draws out the sexy side of you, but if you put

---

How to Bring Out the Bad Boy
in the Good Guy

- Have fun with sexy food, like chocolate-covered strawberries or whipped cream.
- Slip into something more comfortable when you bring him home after a date.
- Introduce ice into your sexplay.
- Let him pin you against the wall.
- Wear something extra racy.
- Let your hand roam while he's driving (hand only—I don't want you getting into an accident!).
- Whisper in his ear what you want him to do to you.
- Tell him you're pretty tipsy and ask if he's going to take advantage of you.
- Ask him about his wildest sexual experience (be prepared to listen without flinching).
- Tell him about your lesbian experience in college.
- Do a striptease instead of making him remove your clothes.
- Fool around in public—a bathroom, a dark alley, a cab, etc.

---

in the work of drawing out your own sexy side, then you won't be as dependent on finding a bad boy.

Believe it or not, there's a bit of bad boy lurking in every guy. You might be thinking that if a guy has a respectable job, shops at Brooks Brothers, and wants to have kids, he's expecting a certain type of behavior from you. But it's in your power to show him that what every guy wants *does exist*: a girl who's both marriageable and fuckable! At the same time, you're letting him show the same thing about himself. But you both might have to loosen up first before he'll share the sexier side of himself. Women tend to make the nice guys wait far longer for sex. Then when they do have it, they act like virtual virgins. Like the thought of anything racier than the missionary position has never even crossed their minds. You don't want to punish him just because he's a good guy. He's a man just like any other. Definitely show him that you're a smart, sensitive, even *nice* girl. But just because you're a good person doesn't mean you need to be a Goody Two-shoes. Surprise him! You should be sexy and show that you're a sexual person regardless of the guy you're with—good guy or bad boy. It's going to bring out his own sexy side if he sees yours, and you'll be able to have the best of both worlds.

FLINGS AND OTHER SUCH THINGS

When most of my clients come to me, they tend to pin too many hopes on sex and put so much importance on it that they don't get enough of it as a result. Which is why I'll sometimes

Rules for Flings

- Use a condom—no exceptions.
- Do not sleep with married men—this won't make you feel powerful, just sleazy and cheap.
- Don't expect to hear from him, even if he takes your number.
- Don't try to date him.
- Don't get emotionally attached (this is the most difficult rule).
- This time doesn't count toward your 15 hours.
- As soon as you meet someone with relationship potential, drop the flings.

Having a fling made me realize the power of my own sexuality. I'd always been in denial about it. If anything, I avoided tapping into my sexuality. So one night, I went out to meet a guy from nerve.com for the sole purpose of having a one-night stand with him. It was so much fun to go out and play the role of sex kitten! We had cocktails and a great dinner, then we got this fabulous hotel room and had an amazing time together. Just that one night helped me learn to be more feminine and sexual. —Janine

give them this very fun homework assignment: Have a fling. This isn't the same as sleeping with a guy you want to hear from again. The guys you have flings with should ideally be the sort you *won't expect* to hear from again, and that should be your intention going in. The primary goal of picking up a guy at a bar or having a wild time when you're on vacation is that it can give you a huge ego boost to have some great sex and feel good about leaving it at that. Especially if you find a guy that you're really attracted to. As Paris Hilton would say, "That's hot!"

Don't spend time worrying about being a slut or a tramp or whatever else you might have been brought up to believe about women who enjoy sex. As long as you use a condom (and your judgment), it's okay to have the occasional fling. In fact, it's good for your confidence and can give you a glow that might come in handy for meeting a more long-term guy. Choose wisely, though. Use your instincts when you're considering a guy for a one-night stand. He should come across as just as nice and sincere as a guy you might want to date. But to make it easy for yourself, it's best to pick a guy that you wouldn't marry. Maybe he's a number of years younger than you, or someone who lives out of town. Whatever works for you in making it clear that you're not that compatible outside the bedroom.

Some clients ask me about "fuck buddies." That's a little more complicated, so I don't advise seeing a just-for-sex guy on a regular basis, unless in your heart of hearts you can promise yourself that you're not going to get emotionally attached. Fuck buddies are certainly appealing because you know you'll have great sex. In fact, if you have a fuck buddy and the sex is not great, lose him.

I had a fuck buddy who was really good for me in a lot of ways because I hadn't had a lot of sex before then. I had this sexual piece in me that he really brought out. We never went out and that was okay with me for a long time. But then we started getting together more often—once a week, then twice a week. I quickly found myself wanting more from him. Then I'd compare other guys I dated to him and no one measured up. I suggested that we go on a real date, but he made it clear that a relationship was something he didn't want. Having to end it was really hard, but I knew I needed to move on in order to find a relationship based on more than just sex. —Olivia

In My Clients' Words

What's the point of a fuck buddy if it's not hot sex?! You also don't need to keep setting the ground rules about protection and the like because you both know the drill, and you can also feel free to do more exploring of each other sexually. However, it's *very* hard for women to avoid getting emotionally attached to a fuck buddy. One client of mine likes to take on younger men as lovers for what she calls "boy toy therapy." It works for her, but not all of us have the cool clarity to stay distanced enough when it comes to hot sex.

LOOSEN UP

Some women complain of simply not being sexual people. I urge you to question that in yourself. Being sexual is just an extension of being sensual, and sensuality is completely within your power to heighten. If you're not that into sex, you should try to get more into sex, because it could be a hindrance to getting into a relationship with a man. It could be due to commitment fears or some issues of the past, but whatever the problem, try to work it out. (You may need the help of a therapist or a coach.) You'll then be better equipped to be happy and to find a healthier relationship.

> **Quick Tip**
>
> *Upscale hotel bars can be a great place to meet an out-of-town guy for a fun night! (Watch the ring finger, though; he may be married.)*

Often, women who are uptight sexually are uptight in other aspects of their lives, too. Are you capable of being happy and having fun? If you constantly deny yourself pleasure, whether it's always turning down dessert or not treating yourself to that great vacation you want, that's sad. Do the things that make you happy, including exploring your sexuality. Buy a vibrator! If *Sex and the City*'s Charlotte—the most uptight person ever—could do it, so can you. Whatever you do, don't rely on a man to come along and find the sexual person buried in you. That's not his job. You need to wake up your own sexual being and warm up without him. I read an article about these Tupperware-style parties for sex products that are all the rage in Middle America and the Bible Belt. The hottest-selling product happened to be a lubricant that makes you feel tingly and aroused. The item turned out to be very empowering to these women because they can arouse themselves rather than rely on their husbands for foreplay.

It's not always the man's job to get you warmed up. If you are already warmed up when you hook up with him, he will be that much hotter for you. If

you strive to become a more sexual person, enjoying sex on your own and becoming self-sufficient in that regard, it is going to make you all the more desirable to men. I once read in *Cosmopolitan* that it's a good idea to masturbate before going to a party or out to a bar. You'll have that satisfied glow—it's a man magnet! Plus, it will make you feel more empowered when you aren't dependent on a man for your sexual pleasure.

Tap into all your senses. Buy a top that feels amazing on your skin. Get some sexy lingerie and *don't* save it for a special occasion! Have a night for yourself. Light some scented candles and play some music that makes you feel good. Take a bath and take your time in it. Then you won't be waiting for a guy to read your mind before you allow yourself to have pleasure. You'll be more in tune with your sensual side, too.

DON'T JUDGE

To make a guy feel more open with you outside the bedroom, you need to make him feel like he can be very open in the

Your Bedroom Etiquette	
Good	**Bad**
Being responsive	Being controlling (unless you're in a dominatrix outfit)
Giggling at his jokes	Laughing at his penis
Moaning and groaning	Crying for any reason
Being open	Being a prude
Acting playful	Acting passive
Showing him what you need	Faking orgasm
Dirty talk	Marriage talk

bedroom. This means you need to appreciate what guys are into sexually. Odds are, you're both going to have different things that turn you on. But instead of holding out for a guy who loves trading back rubs while Enya plays in the background just as much as you do, I suggest you try to see if you can appreciate what guys like. Masturbating is one male habit that women could use more of. A guy will appreciate that you know how to pleasure yourself—nine times out of ten he'll even want to watch. I also advise women to get more comfortable with porn. A lot of women are turned off, even offended, by most of what's out there. But the more comfortable you can become with finding the male mentality sexy, the more sexy you'll become with them. *Give porn a chance!* Over time it might stop grossing you out and start turning you on. Get comfortable with looking at women and see if that's appealing to you. (By the way, if you have an attraction to watching the women, too, it drives men wild!) Try picking up a *Playboy* or catching some of the soft stuff on Cinemax (aka Skinemax) late at night to start. Or find a female-friendly sex shop, like goodvibes.com, where you can buy a DVD that's more designed for women. (Yes! They make porn for women!) You can build your way up to the dirtier kind he likes. Whatever you do, don't feel threatened by porn in any way. Men are very visual. They may like to watch girls onscreen and fantasize, but the reality is that they're with you.

Once you chip away at your inhibitions and broaden your mind a little, you'll find a lot more things sexy than you used to. Down the road, you can start exploring each other's fantasies, and you can get him to pleasure you in just the right way. In the beginning, it's best not to be too demanding in bed, but do make sure to get your needs met. You may get a few kinky requests, like being tied up or spanked or, well . . . you name it. You don't have to say yes to everything, of course, but don't judge him, either. Let him be open with you because that's going to lead to a healthier relationship in which he opens up about nonsexual things, too. If what he asks for is way off the charts of something that you would ever try, then it's probably not a match, but if you're convinced that this is the guy for you, then you have to try to be sexually compatible.

There was an episode on the first season of *Desperate Housewives* when Bree's husband was seeing another woman because he liked to be dominated. Now, there's probably no one better than a tough-as-nails character like Bree to play dominatrix, but since she's so judgmental and controlling, her husband never felt comfortable asking her for such a thing. He got his fantasies fulfilled elsewhere instead because of the shame he suspected she'd inflict on him if he were to ask her. Don't be that way! If he likes to be tied up, or be given a strip tease, or even if likes to wear women's underwear—what's the harm? Wouldn't you rather he do it with you than look elsewhere to have his needs met? If it turns your guy on and doesn't harm you, try to lighten up a little and go with the flow. Remember, sex is the fun part of a relationship. At least, it should be!

*N*ow, *don't run out* and buy a leather jacket and a Harley just yet. Being a cool chick isn't the same as looking like the Fonz. It's about being the ultimate woman. Someone who can hang with the guys and be feminine at the same time. Some men get a little conflicted about what they want out of a woman—the virgin Madonna or the whore—just as women are conflicted about the nice guys versus the bad boys, so show him that you can be more than either of those two types. It's about striking just the right balance between the two. Showing you can be sexual *and* nurturing, available *and* mysterious, vulnerable *and* guarded. If you can successfully show all the different sides of yourself, you'll be the girl that every guy dreams of. Basically, what you're striving for is the exact opposite of all those naggy sitcom wives. It's every guy's worst nightmare to be married to that "annoying kind of woman," who loses all interest in sex as soon as she walks down the aisle, and who is more concerned about whether the trash was taken out than how her husband's day was.

You'll notice when you look at online profiles that a lot of guys say they want a girl who can wear a pair of jeans just as easily as a cocktail dress. Think of that as code for "I want a cool chick." The main character in *Bend It Like Beckham* is a great example. She grows into being a very cool chick in that movie. She's passionate about soccer and not afraid to follow her dream, but she isn't afraid of being vulnerable, either. That cute coach of hers falls madly in love with her, not just because she kicks a ball better than most guys, but also because she *has* the balls to admit her fears to him about disappointing her very traditional parents. She shows her fierce side and her vulnerable side. Plus, she shows her feminine sexy side when she gets all dressed up to go clubbing. She looks great in cleats *and* in a little black dress!

THE KALEIDOSCOPE THAT IS THE IDEAL WOMAN

There was this great commercial jingle for Enjoli perfume in the 1980s. It went like this:

> *I can bring home the bacon*
> *Fry it up in a pan*
> *And never, never, never let you forget you're a man*
> *'Cause I'm a woman—Enjoli!*

How's that for the ultimate cool chick? She's great at her job, nurturing on the homefront, and loves sex. That's what most guys want. And when you can be what guys want, it's very empowering. Plus, you are in a position to get a guy who will be all of those things to you, too.

As you can see, it's not just one thing that makes a chick cool. It's a whole combination. I like to think of a cool chick as a kaleidoscope, with countless facets. Every time you look, you see something new. You don't have to be one thing or another as a woman. You can be an athlete and a girly girl. You can be a good lover and a good wife. You can be great at your job and still want to be a mother. You can be all those things. Our society sometimes pigeonholes women into a certain restrictive definition of being "feminine." I often tell my clients to pick up a few "guy" habits to expand their repertoire a little: Learn to drive stick shift, buy a power drill, become a master at foosball. Stop looking down on him for drinking his milk out of the carton and join him instead. It puts a guy at ease knowing you're not some delicate flower. You're someone he can relate to. At the same time, show your feminine side so you're not actually mistaken for one of the guys. So wear a short skirt while you use that power drill, and you will feel extra powerful! Being warm is cool; so is being sincere and vulnerable. Show your sexy side at the same time. It all sounds complicated, but actually, it's not. Picture yourself making martinis and guacamole while he hangs a shelf for you using your power drill. You show your maternal side by making him food, show an interest in guy things by knowing about bartending and having a power drill, and show your vulnerability by needing his help with the shelves (guys love to be needed). In the end, you both get your needs met, and you come off as the "cool chick." I also tell my clients to learn to flirt better, with men and with women. Being cool is about being in touch with your sexuality and not being repressed in any way. So if a guy says a girl is hot, agree! If you're out with the boys and they want to go to a strip club, go! Draw the line at gyrating onstage, but it's okay to show your wild side. That's part of being cool. It's also very important to show your maternal side, so you have some warmth to go along with all that cool. What do I mean by that? It means being kind and loving, supportive when he's had a bad day, excited for him when he's had a good day. But try to avoid all the "motherly" qualities that are more pushy in nature.

Being Maternal	Being His Mom
You fold his laundry.	You yell at him for leaving his socks on the floor.
You ask how his day was.	You ask when he's going to get promoted.
You let him pick the movie.	You drag him to chick flicks.
You nurture him.	You nag him.
You value his opinions.	You think he should agree with you on everything.
You buy him his favorite cookies.	You buy food you think he *should* like.
You ask for his help to solve problems.	You're one of his problems.
You take him out to lunch.	You tell him what fork to use.

WHAT IS A COOL-CHICK STRATEGY?

Have you seen *An Officer and a Gentleman*? Debra Winger's character plays it cool in that movie. She allows herself to be vulnerable by stating what she needs, but she knows when to walk away. Then in the end, Richard Gere's character literally sweeps her off her feet. The other girl, who fakes a pregnancy to get her guy to marry her, is *not* a cool chick.

GET HIM "THAT INTO YOU."

Remember how everyone jumped on that *He's Just Not That Into You* book? The reason it sold so well was because it was so liberating for a woman to have an excuse like that in her pocket for whenever things went badly. It's easy to blame it on the guy and move on. But there comes a point where you need to figure out *why* he's just not that into you, especially if every guy you date seems to be "just not that into you"! Of course there are guys who aren't in relationship mode and, no matter how cool you are, they wouldn't seem that into you. But if you're really lacking in the cool-chick qualities I've described, you might want to take a personality

> *Whenever I need some "cool-chick" inspiration, I watch an episode of* Buffy the Vampire Slayer *or* Alias. *You just feel fired up after watching them kick ass and look hot at the same time.*
> —Donna

In My Clients' Words

evaluation of yourself. Sit down and see if there's a chance you're being perceived as that "annoying kind of woman" I mentioned. For instance, if you've ever had a boyfriend suddenly leave you and you have no idea why, it might mean you're not a cool chick. There's a chance you just weren't the right fit, but don't let yourself make excuses when your behavior could be a reason why he left, and it's in your power to change. It's possible that there were things about you that bothered the man in your life, but he found it easier to leave than to confront you on it. Even though he wimped out, and it's tempting to blame him for that, he still may have had a point. When you learn to be the cool chick, you'll be able to get him "that into you."

THE THREE EVILS

Just about every annoying habit that a woman has when it comes to men can be broken down into three categories: needy, controlling, and judgmental. I like to call them the three evils.

Needy

You know how I told you that you don't need to talk to a guy every day? That's one of the biggest ways a woman can come across as needy. Why do you really need that, anyway? The truth is, you don't. It's just something you want that you're presenting as a need, and often it's just going to make him want to *run*. Another needy thing is not getting off the phone for an entire hour every time you do speak. You know when you're trying to get off the phone with someone and it's a twenty-minute process? Don't make him feel that way about you, or he won't be eager to call you. John Gray, the author of *Men Are from Mars, Women Are from Venus* talks about something that stuck with me. He says that men are like rubber bands. When you pull away, they get close. When you get too close, they pull away. That's a good analogy to keep in mind.

Too many physical demands can also come across as needy. Always asking for hugs and needing to touch him all the time and insisting on endless PDAs (Public Displays of Affection) is a total turnoff for a guy. You're going to smother him, and that's going to push him away. The key is to make him want you more, not less. Healthy separation is a good thing. If he feels like there's too much pressure on him—whether it's because you always insist on a long, drawn-out good-bye every time you part ways or because you can't make it through more than eight hours without talking to him—it could drive a perfectly good guy away. So try to avoid the need for constant validation. The guy may be capable of a commitment, but he might not want to commit to *that*. Men have a need for space and quiet time, and that doesn't change just because he's met a girl. He's going to think that his needs can't be met in the relationship if your needs are too great. You may ask, "Well, why doesn't he fight for his right? Why can't he tell me I'm being clingy? I could stop if he told me!" Because that's not his job. You need to self-regulate. You can wait all you want for him to talk to you about it, but he's more likely to just stop calling you instead. He'll just bag on the whole thing. Guys tend to take us at face value rather than thinking they can change us. They're not going to bother trying to make us something we're not, just for them. It's easier to bail and find a more compatible woman. Accordingly, you need to change *yourself*, so you can be that "more compatible woman."

Controlling

There are countless ways you can be controlling while dating, whether it's always being the one to decide where to eat dinner, insisting on four days' notice for a date, or forcing him to choose you over his friends when it comes to making weekend plans. Quit that! Even in the very early "polite" stage of dating, there are things you might be doing that can cause a guy concern. If you're playing phone tag, for instance, and you try to narrow down a specific time for him to call, like, "Okay, try me between six and eight on Tuesday," that's controlling. A lot of women think it's being accommodating, but as I said, it's really not. He's going to see through that, and interpret it as pressure. You're forcing his hand, and he knows it. Let a guy call you in his own time, and you'll not only come across as less controlling, you'll get a better sense of what kind of man he is, too. It may be fine to be nitpicky and overexplain things with your girlfriends, since women tend to hyper-communicate, but guys are different. It's okay to play phone tag, remember? And so what if you go to a restaurant you don't like? You have to let him make choices in the relationship or you'll either emasculate him or lose him. Even if you win the argument, you really lose, because most women don't want to be with a castrated (some would say pussy-whipped) guy. Being part of a relationship means you can't be in charge all the time. The sooner you loosen up the reins, the better off you'll be. Cool chicks are not control freaks.

Judgmental

Remember when I told you I didn't allow male bashing? Well there are some subtle ways in which you may still be doing it. Guys do some things we might not be able to relate to, but it doesn't mean we're better than them. So don't judge them. They can be messy, they're often more crass, they're a little more rough around the edges in general. And guess what? They're pretty self-conscious about all that, especially when dating someone new. The more you allow him to be himself around you, instead of hiding his "guy" side, the more he's going to want to be around you. If he burps, laugh. If he swears, don't look horrified. Swear once in a while yourself. Show him that you can handle it and that you're not going to judge him, and he's going to think you're a pretty darn cool chick. You should even imitate some typical "guy" behavior, like drinking beer out of the bottle or telling a dirty joke, just to put him at ease with you. More than anything, a guy wants to feel comfortable around you, so the less he has to hide of himself, the more open he's going to be with you in other ways.

Women also tend to judge a guy's hobbies, whether it's watching sports or porn or playing video games. We discussed

Advice from Dan Aferiat,
Your On-Call Therapist

Is it wrong to want a knight in shining armor?

We all go into relationships wishing that our partners will rescue us from something. Yet no one has the power to rescue anyone from internal fears and conflicts. Being realistic in dating involves coming to terms with that idea. Often, the more loss and trauma that someone has experienced in his or her early life, the more rigidly he or she will hold on to unrealistic fantasies of perfection. As no one can really meet unrealistic ideals, these unrealistic fantasies also act as a perfect defense mechanism, preventing any real form of intimacy or self-knowledge.

the porn situation in the sex chapter, and I hope you'll be more open-minded about that, but try to join in on a few of his other habits, too. If you show him that you can enter into his world, he'll find you more fun to hang with. A lot of women want their guys to be their best friends, but they've never had a guy best friend. It's usually very different than being friends with a woman, so it might take some practice and some loosening up. But if your goal is for your man to be your best friend, you have to learn some stuff about male bonding and what guys are all about. Hint: Guys get together to play—not talk. The guy way often leads to more of a good time, anyway. Playing video games can be a lot of fun, so give it a shot.

I want you to keep the three evils in mind as you go forward in dating. One common mistake women make in relationships is forgetting that men have their own needs and feelings. That's not being a cool chick! Just because a guy doesn't voice his needs and feelings as much doesn't mean that he doesn't have needs or want you to recognize them. Consider your actions and how they might be perceived. Examine and interpret your moves from his point of view. You'll learn a lot. You could think you're pretty cool and accommodating, but you could be doing some things that routinely piss guys off. For example, talking during a movie or always being late. Changing how you come across to men doesn't require an entire personality makeover. It just means making some shifts in your behavior and tuning in a little better to the other person in your life.

PLAYING CEO OF PASSION

Even though women can develop some nasty habits to destroy perfectly good relationships, we still do know a lot about relationships. We have a lot to teach men about how amazing a relationship can be. The best way to teach them is not by explaining it but rather by showing them. You may be disgruntled by the fact that we're more into relationships than men are, but instead of talking to him about it or obsessing about how unfair it is, show your guy that it can be fun. Because you do analyze relationships more than most men and see the value in having a good relationship, use your knowledge to your advantage. Appoint yourself as CEO of passion and consider it your job to keep the passion in the relationship. Think of yourself as Mary Poppins (just don't dress like her) and add a spoonful of sugar to the deal to make him see all the good things about being in a committed relationship. You do it with actions, not words. Instead of saying, "Being a swinging bachelor is bad," show him he can have his cake and eat it, too, by being a cool chick and not a whiny nag! Spice up your relationship by showing the cool, fun, sexy parts of yourself. If he's gun-shy about committing because he's worried his freedom will be in jeopardy, show him it won't be by letting him hang out with his buddies for a weekend without calling you or whatever else he wants to do that has no bearing on your relationship. You can guide him into thinking a relationship is cool once you show him it *can* be cool! If you blatantly pressure him toward a bigger commitment, you're not playing smart or subtle, and he's going to fight you on it. Guide the relationship behind the scenes instead, and you'll have more success.

DON'T BE A PUSHOVER.

Being easygoing and nonjudgmental does not mean you should go along with everything he says. The cool chick is in no way a pushover! If he's exhibiting behavior that you find truly unacceptable, don't accept it! If he spends *all* his time with his friends and blows you off to be with them, for instance, obviously he's the one not being very cool. What do you do in that case? You take a hike. Being a cool chick isn't about rolling over and letting him get his way on everything. It's not about bending over backward to make sure he's happy without doing things to make yourself happy. A cool chick confronts her man to get her needs met, but she is mindful of not being overly needy. A cool chick also takes care of herself and says no to what she doesn't want. If you can successfully be a cool chick with a good guy, he's going to be cool to you and do all he can to make you happy in return.

Notice that being a cool chick isn't just about letting a guy feel comfortable with being a guy or even knowing how to be a guy with him. It's also about showing your own vulnerable side.

Cool Chicks Do	Cool Chicks Don't
Go to strip clubs with their boyfriends	Forbid him to go to his friend's bachelor party
Say stupid things sometimes	Repress their every thought
Make fun of themselves	Act like bitches to other women
Know how to make a mean martini	Expect the guy to make the drinks
Love to dance	Sit quietly in the corner
Laugh often	Look down on a guy for telling an off-color joke
Order shots of tequila	Monitor his alcohol intake
Check out other women with him	Give him shit for noticing a hot girl
Express an interest in the world	Act ignorant
Show that they're smart	Hide the fact they went to Harvard by saying they went to college "in Boston"
Know it's okay to have an argument with a guy	Cry during fights
Let guys hold the door for them	Preach feminism, or anything else

Cool Chicks Do	Cool Chicks Don't
Have successful careers	Need the guy to pay for everything
Like to ride on motorcycles	Yell at him for buying one
Order french fries once in a while	Order a salad, then eat all his fries
Love when a dog jumps up on them	Freak out about getting dirt on their new jeans
Know how to be great hostesses	Think cooking is a chore
Play peek-a-boo with kids	Worry about breaking their nails
Want a man	Need a man
Let their men have poker night	Clean up after poker night
Laugh at guy-humor jokes	Let a guy make fun of their friend

Remember in *Notting Hill*, when Hugh Grant's character thought the movie star Julia Roberts played was far too sophisticated and smooth for him? She had to show him that she was just a kid underneath it all by saying, "I'm also just a girl, standing in front of a boy, asking him to love her." Yes, it was a corny line, but the sentiment is dead-on. Think of him as a boy instead of a man, as well, since he's just as nervous as you are about relationships and being cool enough and everything else. Embrace your nerdy side and let him see that you're not that tough, either. I named my dating café "Drip" because everybody feels like a Drip when they're dating. So embrace it. At a lot of so-called singles bars, people feel compelled to pretend they're not single. Women go to meet men but act like they don't want to meet anyone, focusing on their friends and trying to look cool and aloof. So they leave alone and lonely! There's a difference between being "cool" and being "too cool for school."

If you're still having a hard time imagining what it means to be the cool chick, think back to those pool parties in junior high, where the boys always ended up throwing a girl in the pool. I used to wonder in my nerdy junior high days, "What is it about certain girls that makes the boys want to throw them in the pool?" The boys always went for a particular type of girl. Not the one cowering in a corner, scared to get wet, and not the one prancing around asking to be thrown in. It was always the girl who was just the right combination of flirty, fun, and fearless. She didn't mind being thrown into the pool, but she didn't beg for it, either. Be that girl!

BE THE CHOREOGRAPHER

A cool chick knows how to get what she wants. You know those guys who stretch and yawn just as a ruse in order to put their arm around a girl at the movies? It's like that, only you're orchestrating how the relationship's going—figuring out a way to get your arm around the whole thing. Remember how I taught you earlier about how to position yourself near guys you want to meet? Now you're positioning yourself in the relationship, putting yourself in the best position to get your needs met. There's a subtle and sly way of doing this. One character on *The* OC phrased it as, "You've got to play it hot and cold." You don't want to appear schizophrenic, but it's going to keep him interested if you can change gears between vulnerable and tough. Hot for him, and then a little icy. It's kind of a dance. You get close enough to attract him, then pull away enough for him to pursue you.

PLAYING GAMES

If this all feels like "playing games" to you, it should. There's nothing wrong with playing a game, as long as you're not planning to use him and spit him out. Women always say, "I don't want to play games." But dating *is* a game. Your ultimate goal is to get a guy interested in you, so what you're doing is playing to win. It's like a game of tag where you touch the guy and say, "You're it!" and then you run in the other direction. How else would he know to chase you?

So what does all this mean in the practical sense? Say that in the course of an evening, a guy seems to be losing interest in what you're saying. You've probably been playing it too hot—too eager—so sit back and chill out. Act a little less interested yourself and see what happens. You'll often see him trying a bit harder, wondering how he can get your attention back. Careful it doesn't backfire. Acting less interested does not mean be a bitch! You're still being friendly and flirty, but being slightly withholding. Use what you've learned about how to read men's signals so that you can play off of them. If you're making good eye contact, that's a good sign. The whole night doesn't have to be nonstop talking.

Over the course of a longer period, playing hot and cold means not making two moves in a row. Remember that strategy? If you're pursuing him and he's not responding, you are absolutely not going to fix matters by calling him. Calling him twice or e-mailing twice in a row before he's contacted you is not being the *cool* chick.

WOULD YOU DATE YOU?

Sex appeal is fifty percent what you've got and fifty percent what people think you've got. —SOPHIA LOREN

Take a hard look at yourself and your behavior and ask yourself if you'd be a cool chick to date. Are you demanding? Do you expect too much attention? Are you at all difficult to be around? If so, stop it! You need to put an end to that type of bad behavior or you're going to sabotage every potential relationship you find. Now think of all your great traits and try to replace the bad traits you have with more of the good ones. Are you generous? Understanding? A good listener? These are the kind of qualities you should embrace. You want to be able to say, with confidence, "If I were a guy, I would totally want to date me."

How is your sex appeal? That's a quality a lot of my clients need help in boosting when they come to me. Men are very visual. They want to be able to look at you and be drawn in by that, so think of the little things you can do to make yourself look a little sexier in his eyes. You may think this is just about looks, but it's not. While you should certainly be put together and working with all you've got, there's more to it than looking like Catherine Zeta-Jones or Charlize Theron. Do you look sexy when you eat? Try facing a mirror next time and see what you look like. Pretend you're an actress in a movie and you're very aware of the camera. There are so many things you can do just a bit sexier than what you're already doing, whether it's how you sip a glass of water or how you walk away from him after a date (a little bit of a sway is great). What you do on a date stays in his mind far longer than what you say. You should also try to sound sexier, on the phone and in person. Breathe out a little when you speak, talk more slowly, more softly, more seductively. Shrill = very uncool. You don't want to sound like Janice from *Friends*. That is not sexy! One male client of mine told me that part of his criteria when trying to find the right woman for him was hearing a voice he'd want to hear for the rest of his life.

Attracting the guy you want is about exuding your sexuality and showing interest in a relationship at the same time. You *can* be both sexy and relationship-oriented. It can be the best of both worlds for him, and for you, too! A lot of guys who disappear early on in a relationship are doing so out of fear of what being in a relationship means. Especially if you're putting demands on him as far as how often you see him and how much you contact him. You may think that you have so much fun together you should be seeing each other every day. To him, that feels like you're taking away his freedom. He's now obligated to spend all his spare time with you, and most men would rather keep some autonomy. As much fun as he had with you on your first few dates, being with you is going to seem like a chore if he doesn't have a choice in the matter. A guy's idea of a great relationship is having some freedom and independence. So the more you can embrace his freedom, the better you're going to do. By the way, freedom and independence make for a healthier relationship, anyway. Do you remember what I told you about being the CEO in the relationship? A good CEO looks at the big picture—that both of you should be happy in the relationship. Play your strategy right and you will ultimately have more control, if you don't act controlling. Don't freak out if he wants to have some alone time (i.e., without you) one weekend, or wants to stay home and watch the game instead of going to that "meet the author" event with you at the local bookstore. You still have friends, right? Hang out with them sometimes! The more strict

This guy I'm dating kept saying he wasn't ready for us to have sex, and he seemed to be growing more distant in other ways, too. I asked him about it and he made all these excuses about being too busy and juggling too much. I wasn't going to keep pushing. So finally I said, "Do you even want to be in this relationship? Because I've compromised my own needs in the past, and I'm not going to do that anymore." He got really scared and told me he was sure that I was about to break up with him. I confirmed it. All of a sudden, there was a huge change in him. He opened up and told me that two of his exes each got weird after they had sex and he didn't want to go through that again because it caused them to break up. I think scaring him worked. We ended up having sex the next night. And we've been together ever since. —Karen

you are, the more a guy will fear he can't live up to your high standards, and he'll leave. Remember how pathetic Kevin Spacey's character was in *American Beauty*? He was beaten into submission by his wife, his freedom stolen away right along with his dignity, and that is every guy's worst nightmare. At one stage, his wife (Annette Bening's character) must have been fun and sexy, because she sure is wild when she has an affair with another man. But at some point she stopped being fun and sexy with her husband. She chose to act like a raving bitch with him instead. If a guy forecasts a future like that, you're never going to see him again. A lot of guys worry about that, and it has nothing to do with you. It's just how they think about marriage. It's your job to dispel that myth.

BE WILLING TO WALK AWAY

Finally, in order to be the ultimate cool chick, you have to be willing to walk away from the relationship. You can't decide that he's the One for you before he's proven himself, or you'll never get your way in the relationship. In negotiating, you have no bargaining position if you're not willing to walk away. This isn't something you can fake, either. Now that you know the Program, you know you can get other dates easily, and into another relationship. So always keep that in mind. Remember, men can smell desperation. They don't want you clinging to them like they're a life preserver in some sea of loneliness. If you're really attached and needy, he's going to be less inclined to be interested in you for the long haul. As Conan O'Brien says, "*Be cool, my babies!*"

Finish the Game

There are bound to be times that you're going to get discouraged. Don't consider that a bad sign. Just because things aren't coming together immediately doesn't mean this Program isn't working for you. You can't control every aspect of dating. As I've said, dating is an out-of-control experience by nature. And it takes time and has its ups and downs. Still, having your Cablight on is meant to be *fun!* If you're not having fun at least some of the time, you're missing something and need to change things. Does it still seem like you're always going out with losers? Try aiming a little higher in your search, so you're going out with guys you might actually want to see again. Maybe you're not going after the guys you really want, because the risk of rejection is higher. Choosing losers feels safer, because those guys shower you with attention. But it's not the attention you want, so you have to keep looking.

Even dates with guys you're not interested in can be fun. Turn every experience into something useful and you'll reap more from your efforts. Learn about his career, for instance. Maybe he's an airline pilot and you've always wanted to know the difference between a 757 and a 737. If he's in finance, get some stock tips. Ask him where he has traveled, what restaurants he loves, what music he's been into lately. You might pick

I find that if I listen to some fun "chick songs" it gets me motivated to feel fabulous and get my groove on. Some of my favorite pick-me-ups are:

"Get Ur Freak On" (Missy Elliot)
"Milkshake" (Kelis)
"Rich Girl" (Gwen Stefani)
"Mr. Big Stuff" (Jean Knight)
"I Enjoy Being a Girl" (Rodgers and Hammerstein)

—Lindsay

up some good information. If you're really bored, pretend you're the cabdriver on *Taxicab Confessions* and you're interviewing him. Get better at getting those wild and crazy stories from a guy. You might even find out there's more bad boy to him than meets the eye.

Whatever it takes to make it fun—whether it's practicing new flirting techniques on a guy or finding out some new movies to see—dating shouldn't be this grueling thing that you're constantly dreading. You have to know in your heart that there's a light at the end of the tunnel. Hold onto the belief that there's someone just around the corner. That's why you got this book, right? There's some excitement in that. If there's not, you might need an attitude check. If you think you might be dreading a relationship, either consciously or unconsciously, you should try to explore that, either with a dating coach like me, or with the help of a therapist. Otherwise, stay positive. Don't be afraid to wish for what you want.

MIX IT UP

If you feel like you're doing the same thing every week for your 15 hours and getting the same ho-hum results, you need to change your game. Otherwise, you'll feel like you're on an endless, boring treadmill to your own version of no-man's-land. Instead of going to the local café that feels comfortable to you but that gets no more than two male guests a night (and one of them you suspect is gay), go elsewhere! Push yourself past your comfort zone and take more risks, and you'll get a better hit rate. There's no point in doing stuff that's not working for you. Try some new hobbies to make things more fun for yourself and to widen your net at the same time. Take a martial arts class, start going to art gallery openings, try some bars in other parts of town—do anything to go outside your ordinary haunts. You never know what you might find.

Occasionally, my clients will be afraid to have their regular session with me because they took a break and feel guilty about it (like I'm the Jenny Craig lady about to weigh them). If you take a breather, don't beat yourself up and don't blame yourself. No need to feel guilty. It's okay to take a break here and there during the 6 months if you're feeling demoralized and need to re-group. Just don't leave the Program for more than a week or two or you might lose momentum in your search. But if you've been at this a while and really think you need to take a breather, do it! Make it fun, though. A true refresher is not an excuse to wallow in your sorrow. Indulge yourself by going to a spa or taking a vacation (or both!). It's very important that you keep this process fun for yourself. There's a law of diminishing returns when you become overfocused or obsessed with finding a husband. That's why people think "it happens when you least expect it." You don't want to be impatient with getting the end result. Too much negative attention on a goal can become counterproductive, so just focus on the day-to-day aspect of the search and enjoy the ride. That's a lot of the reason why I ask you to do 15 hours a week. If you are doing 15 hours a week with a positive attitude, you can relax. You're doing your part. You need to save time to do some fun stuff yourself. Get a massage, see a movie, go shopping. You shouldn't be thinking about this 24-7.

PUSH YOURSELF!

I know it can be hard to follow the Program sometimes, especially if you don't have me cracking the whip on you as I do with my clients. If you need to, think of your 15 hours and going on a date a week as an assignment your boss has given you. This assignment is way more important than anything related to your job. Getting into a good relationship is the Number One priority for most women, so learn to crack the whip on yourself! You're reading this book because you know that finding a relationship is crucial to your happiness. So, use your resources of time, money, and energy proportionately. If you constantly let yourself off the hook about meeting men, you might not get to your goal of meeting the One in 6 months or less. That doesn't mean you can't take a coffee break, of course. Just don't isolate yourself or hide by hanging just with your girlfriends or your family. If you sense you need a bit of a break, follow my advice above and take one, then work to get back on the Program. If you keep doing this while you're miserable, you're going be resentful of it. That's not good! As soon as you resign yourself to the fact that your cat's going to be your soul mate, that's going to be a very bad moment in your life. So do all you can to avoid that by keeping your faith in yourself and having a good time. If you know you're lovable, then you will find love. Remember to make "the party that is you" into the blowout bash of the year! Your life is a story where you get to write your own ending. And the people who are invested in having a *happy* ending, will. If you really want this and you're willing to do what it takes, you'll get it.

MY STORY

Finding a relationship was something that was really, really important to me. Yet for a long time, it was something I just couldn't make happen for myself. Like some of you, I'm sure, I had been in a serious relationship that I thought was going to lead to marriage. It lasted three years. When it didn't work out, I felt like I had failed. And I was very depressed and lonely. It took me a while even to want to date again. I was twenty-nine and I felt like my life was over. I felt too old for the bar scene, and it just seemed like I was living the wrong life. I was supposed to be married when I was twenty-seven!

Figuring out my lovelife was so important to me, though, that I actually went to the extreme of creating a business based on it! As they say, necessity is the mother of invention. That's when I created Drip, the café dating service that became famous for helping thousands of people to find love. I created a place to meet great people, figuring I'd start a business and meet a great guy at the same time. Not a bad plan, right? (A lot more work than might have been necessary, but I did get a great career out of it.) I started Drip with little money and less experience, and I ended up making a success of it and getting tons of publicity. But as far as finding the One for me? Three years into Drip, it hadn't happened yet. Partly because I was working too much. Even though I was right in the market, I was off the market because my business was my priority, not my desire to find a husband. I used to make the joke that I was the date-maker that didn't have any dates. But no one ever laughed. Finally, I realized I needed to go outside Drip in order to get out of my comfort zone and to focus on my dating life. I realized it wasn't about the venue or even meeting the right guys, it was about me being ready and about putting myself "out there." I needed to follow my own advice and make dating a priority. It wasn't going to "just happen" until I took matters into my own hands.

Once I came to that decision of putting my personal life on the front burner, I met my husband two weeks later. And I did it by going out alone! I'd made tentative plans with a friend to meet her at an event and she stood me up. Of course I didn't *want* to go out alone, but I knew that it was important to push past my comfort zone, so I went. As I mentioned earlier, I did have an opportunity to meet Dan, now my husband, at the party, but I had flinched and missed my chance. I left after a couple of hours, but something in the back of my head was telling me not to wander too far. A few blocks away, I stopped and made a call from my cell phone. At the same time, I was thinking, "If that guy walks outside right now, it'll be a sign." He did! I thought, "Fate's telling me something." I'd missed my chance the first time, but I wasn't going to miss it again. He looked my way and I smiled at him, which is a hard thing to do with a stranger, especially if you're shy, but I made myself do it. He kept on walking (he was with a friend), but he turned around to look at me. So I knew I had an "in," and I started following him, because I had nothing better to do than follow a guy I liked. He slowed down and stopped at the corner. I said something dumb like, "Oh, you caught me on my cell phone." (Pretty dorky, right?) But it didn't matter what I said. In fact, to this day, *he* claims to have had the opening line. We started walking together and talking like it was totally natural. He took my phone number and called the next day. Five months later, he proposed.

THE CONVERGENCE OF NAMES

You know how weird coincidences happen, where you keep running into the same guy you met at a party three years ago? Or you keep meeting guys named Jason over and over? It doesn't necessarily mean that you're going to marry the guy from the party, or that the guy you end up will be named Jason. But I interpret those things as signs; it's the universe telling you that you're going in the right direction. Like something's saying, "You're on the right path—keep it up."

Of course, you can choose to believe that fate has no hand in what we do, but I believe that there's something bigger than us out there helping along our quests to find our mates. You do have to find your own fate, though. It's not as easy as throwing your hands up in the air and thinking that Cupid will do all your work for you. I actually had to go out to that party, for instance. Alone! And I had to smile at Dan and even follow him down the street to help things along. A speaker I once heard said, "Everything comes down to luck, but you have to be ready to grab it." You have to be able to look for your luck and seize it. Don't let it pass you by! You can't let your fears—or discouragement—prevent you from getting what you want. Believe in the contradiction of having free will and fate at the same time. There's another force operating that you can't control, but you *can* try to follow where it sends you. Try to reach that point in your mind. Believe that it's your fate to have a wonderful guy in your life, and you will. Remember when I warned you about self-fulfilling prophesies? How if you believe you're going to be miserable and alone, you just might? Well, they work in a positive way, too. People who have a genuine belief that it's going to happen for them will find success in my Program.

Sometimes believing in the concept of fate helps when it comes to guys who don't work out, too. When you get dumped, for instance, it helps immensely if you believe that "it wasn't meant to be." You don't look to blame him or yourself, you just accept it and move on. If he didn't want to be with you, why would you think he'd be good for you? Blame it on the universe. And know that someone better is out there, just waiting for you to find him. If fate's telling you this guy's not for you, then believe it. You don't want to think you know better than the universe.

HITTING ROCK BOTTOM

You may be so down on your luck that you can't imagine things ever looking up. Unfortunately, sometimes you have to hit that point before you meet the One. They say, "It's always darkest before the dawn." A lot of people who met and married through Drip told me afterward that right before they met the person for them, they'd hit a point of despair. Usually, though, they had dusted themselves off and told themselves it was all going to be okay and that they were going to keep trying, even though it was incredibly hard sometimes. My clients will often come to me and say, "This is *harrrd*." I am sympathetic, but I don't ever tell them they can just stop working. Most things that we want in life are hard. You think it's easy for Michelle Kwan to win the World Championship figure-skating title every year? Or for a doctor to make it through med school? The Boston Red Sox to have won the World Series? Just because it's hard doesn't mean you can't do it. You've probably done other hard things in your life. I know we've been conditioned to think that finding a guy shouldn't be work in the same way that sports and careers are— it should just be this magical moment that we're all entitled to. But that's just not realistic. Whenever someone tells me that it's hard to put their Cablight on and spend 15 hours a week on the search, and to deal with the inevitable heartache that comes from dating, I say this to them, "I know it's hard. . . . But do it

---

Required Viewing

Here are some of my favorite movies that illustrate my point that everything can turn on a dime. If you are feeling particularly down, go out and rent one for inspiration.

Next Stop Wonderland	*Punch-Drunk Love*
Strictly Ballroom	*Bend It Like Beckham*
When Harry Met Sally . . .	*An Officer and a Gentleman*
Garden State	*Good Will Hunting*
Crossing Delancey	*Working Girl*
Sideways	

---

anyway!" It's not fair, but, again, do you want it to be fair or do you want to be happy? Besides, things can turn on a dime. You could be down on your luck for ages, but then, *Bam!* Suddenly your whole world changes. We all know stories about our "most single" friend, who suddenly finds "the One," and everything changes. It's miraculous to see. Why can't that be you?

AIM HIGH

If you're realistic, you can get everything you want when it comes to the traits you look for in a guy. You shouldn't be overly picky or perfectionistic about it, but you *can* get your dream guy. You can get the combination of being attracted to someone, having great chemistry, a solid friendship, and a true bond. Someone who will be a good father and a good husband. A good guy with a bad-boy side. It will be hard work, and you have to possess many of these types of qualities in return, but it is possible. You shouldn't go into a marriage thinking that you're settling. How depressing would that be?

Give it some time, put in the work, and give guys a chance to prove their worth. Those awesome guys are out there, so don't settle if something is fundamentally not right. (Only you can know what that something is.) If you think you won't be able to tell whether you're being too picky, you'll figure it out soon enough. With this Program you will develop killer instincts and a whole new understanding of what to look for. You'll have experiences that you'll learn from and patterns to draw from. And you'll be in a much healthier place overall. Don't rush this process, either. I know you can't wait to find your man, but it's better to let this take a little longer than you might have wanted than to rush it and perhaps make an error in judgment. You will find a much better relationship in the end if you take your time. My Strategies were not only developed to teach women how to find a relationship, but how to find a *healthy* relationship.

DON'T GIVE UP

The biggest thing I want you to take away from this book is to remain hopeful. You need to be able to know in your heart that a happy, healthy, long-term relationship is in your future. I know I haven't met you, but I firmly believe that just by buying this book, you are telling yourself that you believe your soul mate is out there. You're bound to run into some setbacks along the way, of course. When you meet someone and it starts to look promising and then it doesn't work out, that's nothing short of heartbreaking. I've been there. With every guy I met when I was single, I would think, "Is he the One?" And then I'd be crushed when he wasn't. It can hurt you, discourage you, and deflate your hopes, but I urge you to pick yourself up and move on. Your hopes were right. It's the guy that was wrong. A lot of women will think after breakups: "Oh, I shouldn't have hoped for that. . . . I was wrong in thinking this would come through for me." You were not wrong. The fit was wrong. Now you need to find Mr. Right! By giving you my Strategies, I've handed you everything you need to find a match for yourself. Your job is to make it work for you and to do all you can to turn your Cablight on until you find him. No cutting corners! No doing 5 hours instead of 15. No going on one date a month instead of one date a week, or any other form of cheating. In order to succeed at the Program and find your guy within 6 months, you need to *do* the Program!

Just know that you will get there. Believe it is your fate. Do the work, find your focus, and then relax in knowing that it's going to happen. I remember in high school being so sad and discouraged that I'd never had a boyfriend. I told a friend about it and she consoled me by saying, "Don't worry. It just means your number hasn't come up yet." She gave me a number, like I was in a bakery line. And I felt better. My number came up and so will yours. It's only a matter of time.

About the Author

Nancy Slotnick has a B.A. in Psychological Anthropology from Harvard and she is a professional dating coach with a list of satisfied clients and successful marriages to her credit. She created Drip®, a coffee bar/dating service, which opened in June 1996 on the Upper West Side of Manhattan, and her popular Web site, Cablight.com, offers a range of services and products in the area of lovelife management. Nancy lives in New York City with her husband, psychotherapist Daniel Aferiat, and their son.